EPIDEMICS

OPPOSING VIEWPOINTS®

Mary E. Williams, *Book Editor*

Bruce Glassman, *Vice President*
Bonnie Szumski, *Publisher*
Helen Cothran, *Managing Editor*

**OPPOSING
VIEWPOINTS®
SERIES**

GREENHAVEN PRESS
An imprint of Thomson Gale, a part of The Thomson Corporation

THOMSON
———✳———™
GALE

Detroit • New York • San Francisco • San Diego • New Haven, Conn.
Waterville, Maine • London • Munich

© 2005 Thomson Gale, a part of The Thomson Corporation.

Thomson and Star Logo are trademarks and Gale and Greenhaven Press are registered trademarks used herein under license.

For more information, contact
Greenhaven Press
27500 Drake Rd.
Farmington Hills, MI 48331-3535
Or you can visit our Internet site at http://www.gale.com

Cover credit: Centers for Disease Control and Prevention

LIBRARY OF CONGRESS CATALOGING-IN-PUBLICATION DATA
Epidemics / Mary E. Williams, book editor.
p. cm. — (Opposing viewpoints series)
Includes bibliographical references and index.
ISBN 0-7377-2282-7 (lib. bdg. : alk. paper) —
ISBN 0-7377-2283-5 (pbk. : alk. paper)
1. Epidemics. 2. Communicable diseases—Prevention. I. Williams, Mary E., 1960– . II. Series: Opposing viewpoints series (Unnumbered)
RA652.E645 2005
614.4'973—dc22   2004061657

Printed in the United States of America

"Congress shall make
no law. . .abridging the
freedom of speech, or of
the press."

First Amendment to the U.S. Constitution

The basic foundation of our democracy is the First
Amendment guarantee of freedom of expression.
The Opposing Viewpoints Series is dedicated to the
concept of this basic freedom and the idea that it is
more important to practice it than to enshrine it.

Contents

Chapter 4: How Can Food-Borne Illness Be Prevented?

Why Consider Opposing Viewpoints?

"The only way in which a human being can make some approach to knowing the whole of a subject is by hearing what can be said about it by persons of every variety of opinion and studying all modes in which it can be looked at by every character of mind. No wise man ever acquired his wisdom in any mode but this."

John Stuart Mill

In our media-intensive culture it is not difficult to find differing opinions. Thousands of newspapers and magazines and dozens of radio and television talk shows resound with differing points of view. The difficulty lies in deciding which opinion to agree with and which "experts" seem the most credible. The more inundated we become with differing opinions and claims, the more essential it is to hone critical reading and thinking skills to evaluate these ideas. Opposing Viewpoints books address this problem directly by presenting stimulating debates that can be used to enhance and teach these skills. The varied opinions contained in each book examine many different aspects of a single issue. While examining these conveniently edited opposing views, readers can develop critical thinking skills such as the ability to compare and contrast authors' credibility, facts, argumentation styles, use of persuasive techniques, and other stylistic tools. In short, the Opposing Viewpoints Series is an ideal way to attain the higher-level thinking and reading skills so essential in a culture of diverse and contradictory opinions.

In addition to providing a tool for critical thinking, Opposing Viewpoints books challenge readers to question their own strongly held opinions and assumptions. Most people form their opinions on the basis of upbringing, peer pressure, and personal, cultural, or professional bias. By reading carefully balanced opposing views, readers must directly confront new ideas as well as the opinions of those with whom they disagree. This is not to simplistically argue that everyone who reads opposing views will—or should—change his or her opinion. Instead, the series enhances readers' understanding of their own views by encouraging confrontation with opposing ideas. Careful examination of others' views can lead to the readers' understanding of the logical inconsistencies in their own opinions, perspective on why they hold an opinion, and the consideration of the possibility that their opinion requires further evaluation.

Evaluating Other Opinions

To ensure that this type of examination occurs, Opposing Viewpoints books present all types of opinions. Prominent spokespeople on different sides of each issue as well as well-known professionals from many disciplines challenge the reader. An additional goal of the series is to provide a forum for other, less known, or even unpopular viewpoints. The opinion of an ordinary person who has had to make the decision to cut off life support from a terminally ill relative, for example, may be just as valuable and provide just as much insight as a medical ethicist's professional opinion. The editors have two additional purposes in including these less known views. One, the editors encourage readers to respect others' opinions—even when not enhanced by professional credibility. It is only by reading or listening to and objectively evaluating others' ideas that one can determine whether they are worthy of consideration. Two, the inclusion of such viewpoints encourages the important critical thinking skill of objectively evaluating an author's credentials and bias. This evaluation will illuminate an author's reasons for taking a particular stance on an issue and will aid in readers' evaluation of the author's ideas.

It is our hope that these books will give readers a deeper understanding of the issues debated and an appreciation of the complexity of even seemingly simple issues when good and honest people disagree. This awareness is particularly important in a democratic society such as ours in which people enter into public debate to determine the common good. Those with whom one disagrees should not be regarded as enemies but rather as people whose views deserve careful examination and may shed light on one's own.

8

Thomas Jefferson once said that "difference of opinion leads to inquiry, and inquiry to truth." Jefferson, a broadly educated man, argued that "if a nation expects to be ignorant and free . . . it expects what never was and never will be." As individuals and as a nation, it is imperative that we consider the opinions of others and examine them with skill and discernment. The Opposing Viewpoints Series is intended to help readers achieve this goal.

David L. Bender and Bruno Leone,
Founders

Greenhaven Press anthologies primarily consist of previously published material taken from a variety of sources, including periodicals, books, scholarly journals, newspapers, government documents, and position papers from private and public organizations. These original sources are often edited for length and to ensure their accessibility for a young adult audience. The anthology editors also change the original titles of these works in order to clearly present the main thesis of each viewpoint and to explicitly indicate the opinion presented in the viewpoint. These alterations are made in consideration of both the reading and comprehension levels of a young adult audience. Every effort is made to ensure that Greenhaven Press accurately reflects the original intent of the authors included in this anthology.

Introduction

"Because of their impact on society, a coordinated strategy is necessary to understand, detect, control, and ultimately prevent infectious diseases."
—Georges Benjamin, executive director of the American Public Health Association

Throughout history, epidemics of infectious disease have repeatedly threatened human and animal populations. Bubonic plague killed three-quarters of Europe's population in the fourteenth century. Outbreaks of microbial diseases such as cholera, smallpox, and yellow fever routinely swept through U.S. cities prior to the twentieth century, killing tens of thousands. And as recently as 1918, a devastating three-year influenza pandemic spread across much of the planet, killing up to 50 million people worldwide, including 675,000 people in the United States.

During the twentieth century, however, the advent of modern medicine—including the development of the disciplines of microbiology and immunology, the invention of vaccines and antibiotics, and the establishment of public health agencies—promised to make recurring epidemics a thing of the past. Antibiotics dramatically lowered the incidence of tuberculosis and the death rates from bacterial pneumonia in the developed world. By the latter half of the century, vaccines for dreaded childhood diseases such as polio, measles, rubella, and mumps had helped to reduce the occurrence of vaccine-preventable illnesses to 0.1 percent of all deaths in the United States, Western Europe, and Japan. These successes inspired a leading public health official, U.S. surgeon general William H. Stewart, to proclaim in 1967 that "the war against infectious diseases has been won" and that public health resources should instead be concentrated on chronic noninfectious illnesses such as heart disease and cancer.

Stewart's pronouncement was premature. Infectious disease epidemics remain a significant—and growing—problem in the world. In the past three decades, several dangerous diseases have emerged—some appearing for the first time and others occurring outside of their native regions. Legionnaires' disease, acquired immunodeficiency syndrome (AIDS), Ebola hemorrhagic fever, insect-borne Lyme disease and West Nile virus, food-borne *E. coli* and mad cow disease, and severe acute respiratory syndrome (SARS), are among the most challenging emerging illnesses encountered by epidemiologists and health experts in recent years.

The SARS epidemic of 2003 reveals the special difficulties that international public health officials face in a world of readily available jet travel and political and cultural differences. SARS, a dangerous new form of viral pneumonia, broke out in southern China's Guangdong Province in November 2002. Six people died in the original outbreak, but Chinese officials did not alert global public health agencies about the new illness, nor did they initially attempt to contain it. China's government discourages the broadcasting of bad news, and had actually passed a law in 1996 stating that highly infectious diseases were to be classified as top secret. As a result, the outbreak went unacknowledged for months, enabling it to spread far beyond China's borders. The World Health Organization (WHO) did not learn of the illness until February 2003. By that time, an infected Chinese physician from Guangdong had carried the virus to the city of Hong Kong, where he attended a wedding and spread it to several other guests at the Metropole Hotel. Some of these guests later carried the SARS virus to Vietnam, Singapore, and North America. In the end more than half of the SARS cases in the 2003 outbreak could be traced back to the Metropole Hotel. According to WHO, a total of 8,464 people became infected with SARS in 2002 and 2003. Of these, 799 died.

The SARS epidemic has prompted some health experts to demand that the World Health Organization be given the power to intervene in any nation that fails to take the necessary measures to thwart disease outbreaks. WHO, based in Geneva, Switzerland, was established by the United Nations in 1948 to monitor infectious diseases and help national agencies combat epidemics. As this volume goes to press, however, WHO has no enforcement powers and cannot send its medical personnel to combat potential public health threats without the permission of the host nation.

A new international treaty, say some health experts, could empower WHO to immediately dispatch teams of scientists and clinicians to isolate a disease outbreak before it spreads. As Harvard Medical School professor Jerome Groopman argues, "We need new agreements around public health similar to those [involving] nuclear, chemical and biological weapons." Groopman proposes that those nations that report potential threats to global public health and that grant access to "health inspectors" receive economic and medical aid to eradicate the outbreak. Countries that impede efforts to stop epidemics would then be held responsible for the resulting human costs, states Groopman. But many policy makers, such as James G. Hodge of the Center for Law and the Public's Health, argue that a treaty to fortify WHO would simply be rejected by many nations. "Imagine WHO coming into a state out West and making decisions for the state authorities there," explains Hodge. "I don't think that's going to fly in the United States, and if it won't fly here, how should we expect it to fly in less-developed countries?"

Whether new national and international policies would help to stop the spread of emerging diseases is one of several matters debated in *Opposing Viewpoints: Epidemics*, which contains the following chapters: Do Infectious Diseases Pose a Significant Threat to Humanity? What Can Be Done to Curtail the AIDS Epidemic? Are Vaccines Harmful? How Can Food-Borne Illness Be Prevented? The authors in this volume examine the resurgent problem of infectious disease in the United States and around the world and discuss how governments and individuals should respond to the real and potential threats posed by epidemics.

CHAPTER 1

Do Infectious Diseases Pose a Significant Threat to Humanity?

Chapter Preface

On November 5, 2002, two tourists showed up at Dr. Ronald Primas's office in New York City with fever, swollen glands, and fatigue. The couple, John Till and Lucinda Marker of Santa Fe, New Mexico, informed the physician that a rat on their property had tested positive for plague. When Dr. Primas noticed an additional disquieting symptom—a tender and very painfully swollen lymph gland in Marker's groin—he referred the tourists to Beth Israel Medical Center, where infectious disease experts warned the emergency room staff to isolate the couple as a precaution. Beth Israel immediately contacted the city health department officials, who ordered a series of diagnostic blood tests. When the tests came back positive for bubonic plague, city health commissioner Thomas Frieden hastily organized a press conference to inform the public and relay information regarding the disease's transmission.

Since the September 11, 2001, terrorist attacks and the anthrax attacks that occurred shortly thereafter, the U.S. public has been on edge about the possibility of epidemics sparked by bioterrorism. With the November 2002 cases of bubonic plague being the first that New York City had seen in more than a century, officials were rightly concerned that news about the plague's appearance would stir public anxiety. Indeed, initial media reports seemed geared to provoke fear: Fox News Channel ran "Black Death" as an on-screen headline, and the *New York Times* sported a subhead announcing that "A disease that ravaged medieval Europe reappears."

Bubonic plague understandably creates apprehension because of its disturbing history. A bacterial illness transmitted primarily by fleas and by contact with infected blood or tissue, plague has killed nearly 200 million people in the past fifteen hundred years. The most infamous outbreak started in 1347 and eventually killed 25 million people in Europe and 13 million in the Middle East and China. Today, bubonic plague is containable and treatable with the use of antibiotics. However, untreated bubonic plague can eventually settle in the respiratory system and lead to pneumonic plague, a more dangerous infection. While bubonic plague is not transmissible from person to person, pneumonic plague is. And when treatment for pneumonic plague is delayed for more than twenty-four hours, the fatality rate is high.

Theoretically, pneumonic plague can also be transmitted during a bioterrorist attack using an aerosolized form of the bacteria. For this reason, New York health officials decided to initiate a bioterrorism response plan just in case the November 2002 incident proved to be of terrorist origin. Their quick actions enabled the health department and the Centers for Disease Control and Prevention to exclude pneumonic plague as the cause of illness within forty-eight hours of the patients' admissions. As soon as possible, officials were able to inform the public that the couple's form of plague was not contagious. Consequently, in spite of intensive media focus on the cases, the public was not unduly alarmed. Medical experts praised the city's response to the incident as swift and appropriately cautious.

In an age of new and reemerging diseases, separating accurate information from hype can be challenging. The authors in the following chapter share additional insights on the threat of epidemics as well as the dangers of public overreaction to disease outbreaks.

"We [are] less adept at recognizing and effectively dealing with the factors that facilitate the spread of viral and bacterial agents."

The Threat of Infectious Disease Is Serious

Jennifer Brower and Peter Chalk

Modern trends have greatly increased the threat of infectious disease around the world, argue Jennifer Brower and Peter Chalk in the following viewpoint. Increased global trade and international travel as well as an upsurge of people moving to crowded urban areas with poor sanitation inevitably hasten the spread of disease. In addition, the authors point out, modern medical practices such as the use of antibiotics have unwittingly sparked the evolution of powerful and resistant bacteria. Global warming is yet another factor influencing the spread of disease, as higher temperatures are expanding the regions in which dangerous microbes thrive. Brower is a policy analyst at RAND, a nonprofit think tank that assists corporate and government decision makers. Chalk, a political scientist at RAND, is an expert on international terrorism and emerging global threats.

As you read, consider the following questions:

1. According to the authors, what are some recent examples of animal diseases that have "jumped" across the species lines to infect humans?
2. According to Joshua Lederberg, cited by the authors, how is contemporary medical research contributing to the threat of infectious disease?

Jennifer Brower and Peter Chalk, *The Global Threat of New and Reemerging Infectious Diseases: Reconciling U.S. National Security and Public Health Policy*. Santa Monica, CA: RAND, 2003. Copyright © 2003 by RAND. Reproduced by permission.

The bubonic plague that swept across Europe during the Middle Ages, the smallpox that was carried to the Americas by the Spanish, and the influenza outbreak of 1918 all bear testimony to the historic relevance of infectious pathogens and their ability to cause widespread death and suffering. In many ways, however, the nature and magnitude of the threat posed by infectious pathogens are greater today than they have ever been in the past, developments in modern science notwithstanding. Emerging and reemerging infections present daily challenges to existing medical capabilities. Not only have deadly and previously unimagined illnesses, such as AIDS, Ebola, Creutzfeldt-Jakob disease, and Legionnaires' disease, emerged in recent years, but established diseases that just a few decades ago were thought to have been tamed are also returning, many in virulent, drug-resistant varieties. Modern manifestations of TB, for instance, bear little resemblance to the 19th-century strains that haunted Europe. TB treatment now requires a daily drug regimen that often requires health workers to personally monitor patients to ensure that they are complying with necessary procedures.

In many ways, this situation is a result of the natural balance of forces between people and infectious organisms. By one estimate, there are at least 5,000 kinds of viruses and more than 300,000 species of bacteria that challenge human beings, many of which are able to replicate and evolve billions of times in one human generation. These disparities clearly work to the advantage of pathogens, enabling the evolution of ever more virulent strains that quickly outstrip the ability of humans to respond to them. Just as important, however, are "artificial" disease force-multipliers, which are serving to greatly exacerbate the incidence and spread of infectious microbes. Foremost among these are globalization, modern medical practices, accelerating urbanization, climatic change resulting from global warming, and changing social and behavioral patterns. . . .

Globalization

The present international system is now more globally interdependent than at any other time in history. Today one can physically move from one part of the world to another in the same time (if not more rapidly than) it used to take to journey between cities or counties. Indeed, no part of the planet remains inaccessible to human penetration, with current estimates of the number of people crossing international frontiers on board commercial flights at more than 500 million every year. . . .

Whether measured on the basis of information flows, the total volume of world trade and commerce, contact between governments, or links between people, the figures all show major increases, especially over the last 20 years. While it is not necessary to spell out these developments in terms of specific statistics—the trends are both clear and well known—the consequences for the spread and emergence of infectious diseases do require some elucidation.

On one level, the global trade in agricultural products has increasingly brought people into contact with exotic and foreign animal diseases that have subsequently "jumped" across the species line to infect humans. Several examples stand out. In September 2000 a major outbreak of Rift Valley fever hit Saudi Arabia, killing several dozen people in a matter of days. The source of the epidemic was eventually traced back to imports of infected sheep from neighboring Yemen. In Europe, the emergence of the nervous system disorder Creutzfeldt-Jakob disease has been linked to the consumption of beef products originally derived from British cattle afflicted with bovine spongiform encephalopathy, or "Mad Cow Disease." And in the United States, the outbreak of West Nile virus in 2000 is now believed to have originated at least partly from the importation of chickens into New York.

On a more direct level, the speed of modern air transportation has greatly facilitated the global transmission of disease among humans. Travelers experiencing either fully developed or incubating endemic or emerging diseases from their departure location can rapidly carry microbes into nonendemic areas. In the United Kingdom and the United States, for instance, there have been numerous cases of people living near major metropolitan airports contracting malaria apparently imported aboard jets operating transcontinental routes. Equally as indicative is typhoid fever. Roughly 400 cases of the disease are reported every year in America, 70 percent of which are acquired by individuals while traveling overseas. Outbreaks of Legionnaires' disease have been similarly linked to such dynamics. . . .

Compounding the problem is the fact that overcrowded, poorly ventilated, and (sometimes) unsanitary aircraft constitute ideal environments for the transmission of viruses and bacteria, particularly on long flights. Reflecting this, travel health guidelines issued by the World Health Organization (WHO) now specifically refer to the possibility of catching infectious TB in flight as "realistic," especially on flights of more than eight hours. The WHO has recorded several instances in which individuals flying on planes with other TB-infected travelers have been infected with the bacterium that causes the lung infection.

One disease that has certainly reached pandemic proportions at least partly as a result of globalization and the international movement of goods and people is AIDS. Studies in Africa have tracked the progress of the causative HIV agent along trucking routes, with major roads acting as principal corridors of viral spread between urban areas and other proximal settlements. In one study of 68 truck drivers and their assistants, 35 percent were found to be HIV-positive. Further epidemiological research revealed a wide travel history for these individuals, involving seven different countries served by the ports of Mombassa, including Kenya, Uganda, Zaire, Burundi, and Rwanda. Tourism, especially tourism involving sex, has also played a contributing role. There can be little doubt that the global spread of AIDS has been encouraged by the substantial patronage of the Asian sex markets and by the equally large number of international travelers visiting such countries as Thailand, India, and the Philippines every year.

Modern Medical Practices

During the 1960s and 1970s, there was a great deal of hope that humankind had tackled some of its worst infectious diseases through medical advances. This sense of confidence culminated in 1978 when the member states of the United Nations (UN) signed the Health for All, 2000, agreement. The accord set out ambitious goals for responding to infectious diseases among other things, predicting that at least some of the world's poorest and least developed states would undergo a fundamental (positive) health transition before the end of the century.

The optimism inherent in the UN declaration rested on the belief that advances in antibiotics, vaccines, and other remedial treatments—together with striking improvements in food preparation and water treatment—had provided the world's politics with a formidable armory that could be brought to bear against microbial agents. Indeed, just the year before, the WHO had announced the effective eradication of the smallpox virus after the last known case of smallpox had been tracked down and cured in Ethiopia.

Diseases Without Borders

Every day, one million people cross an international border. One million a week travel between the industrial and developing worlds. And as people move, unwanted microbial hitchhikers tag along. In the nineteenth century, most diseases and infections that travelers carried manifested themselves during the long sea voyages that were the primary means of covering great distances. Recognizing the symptoms, the authorities at ports of entry could quarantine contagious individuals or take other action. In the age of jet travel, however, a person incubating a disease such as Ebola can board a plane, travel 12,000 miles, pass unnoticed through customs and immigration, take a domestic carrier to a remote destination, and still not develop symptoms for several days, infecting many other people before his condition is noticeable.

Laurie Garrett, *Plagues and Politics: Infectious Disease and International Policy,* ed., Andrew T. Price-Smith. New York: Palgrave, 2001.

While scientific progress has certainly helped to mitigate the effects of certain infectious ailments, overuse and misuse of antibiotics—both in humans and in the agricultural produce they consume—has contributed to a process of "pathogenic natural selection," which is helping to generate ever more resilient, resistant, and powerful disease strains. Much of this evolution stems from the rapidity with which microbes are able to adapt and replicate plasmid in their DNA and RNA codes, the genetic dynamic of which commands mutation under stress. Individuals who fail to complete prescribed treatment courses further aggravate the problem by allowing a residual, more resistant viral or bacterial base to survive and flourish. . . .

Modern medical science and/or associated practices are helping to heighten human vulnerability to viral and bacterial pathogens in other ways. Invasive treatment procedures are exposing people to hospital-acquired infections, including the [highly resistant] *S. aureus* bacterium. . . . This is particularly true in the developing world, where typically only the sickest—and, therefore, the most vulnerable—are hospitalized. The use of contaminated blood to make clotting agents and antibody plasma proteins such as gamma globulin has similarly exposed patients to highly debilitating diseases such as AIDS and hepatitis C—a problem becoming especially prevalent in China, where there exists a thriving illegal trade in blood.

Just as serious are the nature and direction of contemporary medical research, which is exhibiting an increased predilection toward the wholesale eradication (rather than control) of microbial organisms. Significantly, much of this exploratory work is proceeding in the absence of a definitive understanding of the etiology of diseases and the environmental contexts in which they exist. As Joshua Lederberg, a Nobel prize–winning biologist, points out, this is liable to prove a highly costly (and misplaced) "war of attrition" in that it will probably merely upset the delicate ecological balance between microbes and their human hosts and, in so doing, exacerbate overall individual vulnerability to pathogenic infections and mutations.

Further, improved medical practices have extended the lives of many ill people whose immune systems are less capable of combating microorganisms. An increasing number of individuals in the United States and elsewhere are living with HIV/AIDS infection, cancer, transplanted organs, and aged immune systems. The presence of these people raises the likelihood that opportunistic pathogens will take hold.

Accelerating Urbanization

At the turn of the 20th century, only 5 percent of the globe's inhabitants lived in cities with populations over 100,000. By

21

the mid-1990s, more than 2.5 billion people resided in metropolitan centers. Most of this urban growth has taken place in the poorer parts of the world. In 1950, for instance, roughly 18 percent of the population of developing states lived in cities. By 2000, the number had jumped to 40 percent, and by 2030 it is expected to reach 56 percent. Several of these conglomerations will have populations in excess of ten million inhabitants. Indeed, according to the UN, 24 so-called "megacities" have already surpassed this demographic threshold, including Jakarta, Calcutta, Lagos, Karachi, and Mexico City.

The reasons for the high rate of rural-urban migration throughout the developing world are complex and varied. However, they typically incorporate factors such as drought, flooding, and other natural disasters; an excess of agricultural labor; sociopolitical unrest generated by civil war; a lack of employment opportunities; and rural banditry. Fleeing these types of conditions (or variations of them), millions of dispossessed workers have moved to squalid shantytowns on the outskirts of major third-world cities, swelling urban populations and overloading already inadequate water, sanitary, medical, food, housing, and other vital infrastructural services. These expanding metropolitan hubs are proving to be excellent breeding grounds for the growth and spread of infectious bioorganisms. According to one study, a lack of clean water, sanitation, and hygiene alone account for an estimated 7 percent of all disease-related deaths that occur globally.

Asia in particular has been severely hit by the negative interaction between unsustainable city growth and disease spread. The region's urban population is currently estimated to be 1.1 billion. By 2025, it is expected to have risen to 3.8 billion and Asia will contain half the world's people—more than half of whom will live in cities. Nine of the aforementioned "megacities" already exist in the region, including Beijing, Calcutta, Jakarta, Mumbai (formerly Bombay), Osaka, Shanghai, Tianjin, and Tokyo. . . .

The infectious consequences of these developments are inevitable, with widespread outbreaks of typhoid, malaria, dengue fever, dysentery, and cholera a common occurrence. As [social critic and science writer] Eugene Linden observes:

Advances in sanitation and the discovery of antibiotics have given humanity a respite from the ravages of infectious disease. But many epidemiologists [now] fear that this period is drawing to a close as urban growth outruns the installation of sanitation in the developing world and resilient microbes discover opportunities in the stressed immune systems of the urban poor.

Unsustainable urbanization can affect the spread of disease in other ways. Rapid intrusion into new habitats has disturbed previously untouched life forms and brought humans into contact with pathogens and contaminants for which they have little, if any, tolerance. Mushrooming cities in the developing world are also helping to transform oceans into breeding grounds for microorganisms. Epidemiologists have warned, for instance, that toxic algal blooms, fed by sewage, fertilizers, and other industrial and human contaminants from coastal metropolises in Asia, Africa, and Latin America contain countless viruses and bacteria. Mixed together in what amounts to a dirty "genetic soup," these pathogens can undergo countless changes, mutating into new, highly virulent antibiotic strains that can be quickly diffused by nautical traffic. The devastating cholera epidemic that broke out in Latin America in 1991, for instance, occurred after a ship from Asia unloaded contaminated ballast water into the harbor of Callao, Peru. The epidemic, which originated from a resistant strain of the El Tor serogroup, subsequently spread to neighboring countries, infecting more than 320,000 people and killing 2,600.

Global Warming

Over the past century, humanity has dramatically affected the global biosphere in deep and complex ways. One important effect of such actions has been a gradual increase in the earth's average surface temperature, a change that many scientists now believe has the potential to actively contribute to the transnational spread of disease. According to two 2001 UN studies by the Intergovernmental Panel on Climate Change, the earth's temperature could rise between 1.4 and 5.8 degrees Celsius over the 1990 average surface temperature during the next century.

Global warming could expose millions of people for the

first time to malaria, sleeping sickness, dengue fever, yellow fever, and other insect-borne illnesses. In the United States, for instance, a slight increase in overall temperature would allow the mosquitoes that carry dengue fever to survive as far north as New York City. Also, the insects that carry the *Plasmodium falciparum* parasite, which causes malaria, thrive in the warm climates of the tropics. Increased temperatures in more temperate areas could, conceivably, provide a habitat suitable for the increased distribution of these anopheline vectors. . . .

Global warming and climatic change may also influence the spread of disease by potentially increasing the incidence and magnitude of natural disasters such as landslides, storms, hurricanes, and flooding. Just as in war and conflict, these events invariably lead to the destruction/ disruption of vital communication, health, and sanitation infrastructure as well as the displacement of people into overcrowded, makeshift shelters and camps. Such consequences are likely to have direct adverse effects on public health, transforming a disaster area into a potential "epidemiological time bomb." . . .

Changing Social and Behavioral Patterns

Changes in human social and behavioral patterns have had a profound impact on the spread of infectious illnesses. HIV/ AIDS represents a case in point. Although the precise ancestry of HIV is uncertain, early transmission of the disease was undoubtedly facilitated by greater acceptance of multiple sexual partners and permissive homosexuality, particularly in nations such as the United States. Today, almost 1.4 million people are living with HIV throughout North America and Western Europe, with some cities, such as New York, among the places in the world where the disease is most prevalent. While the rate of new infections in the developed world slowed during the 1990s (especially in the United States)— largely because of the initiation of effective sex education campaigns and the availability of effective antiretroviral drugs—the disease continues to decimate Africa and South/Southeast Asia. Sub-Saharan Africa has been particularly badly affected, where a staggering 21.8 million people have died since the disease was first diagnosed in the early 1980s. Overall, the subcontinent accounts for roughly 70 percent of the world's AIDS cases and three-quarters of its AIDS-related deaths.

In Thailand, Cambodia, and India, thriving sex industries have served to compound already serious problems stemming from greater sexual promiscuity. More than 100,000 cases of AIDS were reported in Thailand between 1994 and 1998. Although an intensive campaign initiated by the government has helped to slow the overall rate of new infections in major centers such as Bangkok, the disease remains a serious problem in northern cities such as Chiang Rai, where roughly 40 percent of female prostitutes are thought to be HIV positive. In Cambodia, nearly half of *all* the country's sex workers are known to be infected by HIV, which causes AIDS. Based on current trends, a staggering 10 percent of the country's population could be infected by 2010. Figures for India are equally as serious. In Mumbai alone, 75 percent of the city's 60,000 to 70,000 prostitutes have contracted the disease, up from just 1 percent in 1990. In total, roughly 3.5 million people are currently thought to be living with the disease in India, a rate of infection that owes much to commercial sex and the high levels of sexually transmitted diseases (STDs) in the country. . . .

The increasing prevalence of intravenous drug use has also been instrumental in encouraging the spread HIV/AIDS. Burma, for example, which sits at the heart of the infamous opium-producing "Golden Triangle" and was free of HIV only a few years ago, now has an estimated 200,000 people carrying the virus, 74 percent of whom are intravenous drug users. Equally indicative is India, where intravenous drug use is now the second most common method of transmission for the disease (behind heterosexual sex), something that is especially true in the northeast regions that border Burma. China has been especially hard hit. The Beijing government freely admits that the outbreak of an AIDS epidemic in the country's south is directly related to drug addicts sharing needles to inject heroin. . . .

Although HIV/AIDS is the clearest example of how altered social and behavioral patterns have affected the occurrence and spread of infectious disease, it is not the only one.

Changes in land use have also played a significant role. The emergence of Lyme disease in North America and Europe has been linked to reforestation and subsequent increases in the deer tick population, while conversion of grasslands to farming in Asia is believed to have encouraged the growth of rodents carrying hemorrhagic fever and other viral infections. In the United States and United Kingdom, the development of large-scale factory farms and increased interactions between rural and urban populations have been linked to outbreaks of *Salmonella* and cryptosporidiosis as well as the general increased incidence of zoonotic diseases that are passed from livestock to humans.

Finally, as society has moved into habitats requiring environmental modification, niches have been inadvertently created that are proving to be highly conducive for microbial growth and development. Heating and ventilation systems using water cooling processes, for instance, are now known to provide the perfect breeding ground and dissemination pathway for *Legionella pneumophila*, the causative agent of Legionnaires' disease.

Medical science has come a long way in improving our basic understanding of the origin and effect of most infectious diseases humans may contract. Nevertheless, we have proven far less adept at recognizing and effectively dealing with the factors that facilitate the spread of viral and bacterial agents. Through such things as urbanization, climatic change, changing social and behavioral patterns, globalization, and misappropriate/misguided remedial procedures, humanity is rapidly approaching what one commentator has referred to as the "twilight of the antibiotic era." Not only are we having trouble controlling age-old problems like TB, cholera, and malaria, but new, previously unimagined illnesses and viruses such as HIV/AIDS have emerged with a vengeance.

*"New media technologies are accelerating
public anxiety about viruses even faster
than new health technologies have
enhanced our ability to cope with them."*

The Media Exaggerate the Threat of Infectious Disease

David Baltimore

In the following viewpoint David Baltimore argues that the
media can cause the public to overreact to the threat of disease outbreaks. In particular, newer forms of media —such as
the Internet and satellite-enhanced television news—often
ply the public with twenty-four-hour coverage of emerging
threats. The fears and anxieties stirred by such media coverage could become more dangerous than the outbreak itself,
Baltimore writes. While openness and access to information
are necessary tools in confronting infectious diseases, the
media should strive to be careful and balanced in reporting
on new outbreaks. Baltimore, a Nobel laureate in medicine,
is president of the California Institute of Technology in
Pasadena, California.

As you read, consider the following questions:

1. How did Americans overreact to the SARS outbreak in
   2003, according to Baltimore?
2. According to the author, how did many people respond
   to the anthrax bioterrorism scare of late 2001?
3. In Baltimore's opinion, who should be responsible for
   educating the media about public health issues?

[In the spring of 2003] Restaurants sit empty in China-towns. Parents keep children home from school in Toronto. Asian hotels and airlines reel at dramatic drops in bookings. Just as the media recently gave us a new and particularly intimate experience of war, we're now getting a new and particularly fearsome experience of a public health crisis with SARS—in which a media-transmitted epidemic of concern for personal safety outpaces the risk to public health from the actual virus.

To be sure, SARS, or severe acute respiratory syndrome, presents serious challenges. It has likely emerged after circulating within some animal species for a long time. It is one of a large number of such viruses that suddenly infect the human populations. Most burn themselves out (although Ebola still smolders in Africa, being particularly devastating to the great ape population). SARS may be worse because it is transmitted more easily, now perhaps through persistence after drying onto surfaces, making it harder to contain. Although much less lethal than HIV, it may therefore be the next virus to settle into the human population. That SARS may always be with us is a possibility we must be prepared to cope with.

But that doesn't mean its effects are not manageable. Given what's happened thus far, the appropriate response is to pursue targeted and aggressive public health measures, while the 99.9% of us not conceivably at risk go on with our lives.

Containing Biological Threats

This is where China's shocking cover-up has proven so costly. In any viral outbreak, early identification and containment is essential. It was our inability to spot and contain HIV that has led to the epidemic of more than 45 million infected people that the world faces today. Now that the Chinese leadership seems to be belatedly cooperating, the world community's overriding objective must be to stop SARS from achieving a similar trajectory.

There is good news in this regard. Advances in technology have helped health professionals get a fix on SARS much sooner than with previous viruses. It took years to identify and isolate HIV. Now, "libraries" of known viruses are stored on computer chips, letting researchers identify suspect strains in a matter of days—a key to devising accurate tests and effective treatments. This progress, related partly to the post-9/11[1] focus on bioterror, suggests that defense-related technology spin-offs may soon be as frequent a boon to public health as they've long proved in aviation or electronics. As we mobilize for faster action against biological threats, it will prove as helpful when germs attack via nature as when they come from the diabolical schemes of terrorists.

The Danger of Too Much Openness

Yet herein lies a tension. The chief means of avoiding an HIV-style scenario are strong and open public health measures. Openness, however, breeds fear and overreaction. This risk has to be managed by careful reporting and characterization—a challenge for the media that may be as thorny as that facing health officials. Indeed, it's arguable that new media technologies are accelerating public anxiety about viruses even faster than new health technologies have enhanced our ability to cope with them. The Internet, e-mail, and satellite-enabled saturation media coverage have put public fear on steroids—and lent a dark twist to the old dot-com hype about the promise of "viral marketing." As a result, people from Guangdong to Greenwich Village hunker down with herbal remedies, thanks to baseless rumors that these offer protections—or that they need protection in the first place.

The de facto boycott of Chinese restaurants across America is the most alarming overreaction, since there's absolutely no reason to think SARS can be transmitted through food, or by people who happen to be Chinese. Your chances of being killed by SARS are remote compared to the chance you'll be killed in your car on the way to a Chinese Restaurant. But media viruses are immune to rational inoculation. The anthrax scare of late 2001 was the preview.[2] With Tom Brokaw and the Senate involved, it was no time before well-to-do mothers added stocks of Cipro and gas masks to the inventory of the compleat parent. That this anthrax episode

---

1. a reference to the September 11, 2001, terrorist attacks on the United States 2. In the fall of 2001, envelopes containing anthrax spores were mailed to several media and government addresses, resulting in five deaths.

29

claimed five lives—when each year 40,000 Americans die in highway crashes, 400,000 from tobacco-related illnesses and 20,000 from flu—doesn't seem to allay fears.

Wright. © 2003 by Larry Wright. Reproduced by permission of Daryl Cagle for Slate.com.

Scientists often complain that the public deals with danger not as a matter of statistical probability but as a function of media exposure. People fear whatever scary new thing TV shoves under their noses. But those of us professionally devoted to rational analysis need to do more than wag our fingers now that the press routinely swells the fear factor toward a level that could itself become a danger.

Striking a Balance

The power of these new "media viruses" presents a paradox. The press does perform a great public service by making virtually everyone on the planet aware of important information overnight. This raises the odds that authorities will take action, or be held accountable if they fail to. In the age before satellite televisions, for instance, it might have taken Chinese leaders many more months (and untold more SARS deaths) to begin to do their duty. But public health professionals may soon learn what those who conduct foreign policy know already: The distorting magnification of the modern media lens brings new risks as well.

This is an aspect of public health crises that our leaders can no longer ignore, and one for which scientists in particular have a special responsibility to educate the media. On a recent "Nightline," Ted Koppel provided a model for such discourse, framing the SARS discussion as a matter of thinking intelligently about the threat in light of the reality that this new disease's reach is far, far smaller than countless other risks we face routinely. The daily press should likewise reassure the public by highlighting this broader context of risk even as it shares that latest scary-sounding news.

We need to improve at striking this balance now. As the SARS overreactions suggest, the era in which public alarm can soar out of proportion to genuine risk is only beginning.

*"Biological weapons readily lend themselves
. . . to catastrophic effects."*

Bioterrorism Is a Serious Threat

Richard Danzig

The threat posed by terrorists' use of biological weapons war-
rants serious attention, argues Richard Danzig in the following viewpoint. A biological attack can kill large numbers of
people, and the technology for building biological weapons is
less expensive and more accessible than the resources required
for other weapons of mass destruction, Danzig points out. In
addition, biological weapons such as anthrax are easy to con-
ceal and offer the possibility of readily repeatable attacks. The
United States should make preparations to defend itself
against a campaign of recurring bioterrorist attacks, Danzig
concludes. Danzig, a former secretary of the navy, is a consultant to several U.S. Department of Defense agencies.

As you read, consider the following questions:
1. What is the phenomenon of "reload," according to
   Danzig?
2. According to the author, how many people could be
   killed by one gram of anthrax spores?
3. In Danzig's opinion, why should the United States plan
   to defend against a campaign of bioterrorism, rather
   than just an attack?

Richard Danzig, *Catastrophic Bioterrorism—What Is to Be Done?* Washington, DC:
National Defense University, 2003. Reproduced by permission of the Center for
Technology and National Security Policy, National Defense University.

A number of studies have identified American vulnerabilities to terrorism. Around the globe, terrorists have attacked airplanes, ships, trains, buses, office buildings, embassies, markets, theaters, resorts, monuments, government officials, businesspeople, and individuals who simply happened to be in the wrong place at the wrong time. Rarely have such attacks involved biological weapons. Why then do these weapons warrant extraordinary attention?

The Threat of Biological Weapons

Many have observed that biological weapons are "a poor man's atomic bomb." A single biological attack can kill a great many people, while the technologies to develop and deliver these weapons are relatively inexpensive, accessible, and difficult to detect, much less interdict. However, an additional attribute of bioterrorism would, if commonly recognized, amplify these concerns. I call this phenomenon "reload." To understand it, contrast the 9/11 [September 11, 2001], air hijacking attacks with the anthrax letters that followed in the fall of 2001 and even more pointedly with the outdoor (aerosol) biological attacks that could occur in the future.

After inflicting a national trauma on 9/11, the attackers could not promptly repeat their achievement. They had consumed resources that were difficult to replenish (trained pilots willing to sacrifice themselves). Even more significantly, the modality that they used depended, in some measure, on surprise. Once alerted to this technique, we had some ability to counter it. Passengers on the fourth 9/11 aircraft fought back. (Months later, passengers and crew similarly overpowered a terrorist attempting to set off a bomb concealed in his shoe.) National authorities could (and did) ground airliners. Later, we flew fighter aircraft over our cities. In the longer term, we took security measures that significantly impede hijacking. As a result, any further attacks of this magnitude will probably need to employ different weapons in a different manner.

When the anthrax letters were mailed, 11 people contracted inhalational anthrax, 5 of whom died. Call this "5/11." Although the number of casualties was limited, the national security vulnerabilities made apparent by 5/11 are

33

greater than those associated with 9/11. This is because of reload. Attackers who use biological weapons probably can avoid prompt detection and stockpile or replenish resources that permit repeated attack. Making a gram of readily aerosolized anthrax spores in a weaponized 1-to-5-micron range is a technical challenge, but, once production is accomplished, it is a much lesser challenge to make 1 kilogram. And it is not a significant challenge for a terrorist organization that can make a kilogram to make 10 or 100 kilograms. Nor, absent exceptional luck, do we have effective means of interdicting a biological attack, even if we know that one has already occurred and that others are on the way. This is especially true with respect to outdoor (aerosol) attacks. While we can shut down our mail system (with great economic consequence—think how taxes and bills are paid and parcels are shipped), we cannot shut down the atmosphere.

The Power of Reload

The gram of anthrax mailed to Senator Patrick Leahy reportedly contained one trillion spores of anthrax. Since inhalation of 8,000 to 10,000 spores is generally regarded as likely to be lethal for the average person, a gram perfectly effectively and efficiently disseminated outdoors under optimum weather conditions and inhaled by an unprotected population theoretically could kill 100,000 people. Outdoor dissemination in liquid or powder form would not be difficult. Of course, a perfectly efficient distribution and exposure rate would not be achieved. All calculations of infection and lethality associated with biological weapons are uncertain, but a reasonable approximate planning premise is that a gram of anthrax released in an urban area might expose between 100 and 1,000 people to a lethal dose. A kilogram (containing 1,000 trillion spores) could be anticipated to infect tens of thousands of people.

The ability to reload and repeat an attack obviously amplifies the number of potential victims. An attacker, having disseminated anthrax one evening in Washington, for instance, could do the same thing the next day in Detroit, Chicago, or Los Angeles. We are very unlikely to observe the act of attack. A terrorist can surreptitiously disseminate anthrax from any of an immense number of points upwind from a target. Even if detectors (a scarce resource) are in position and operating, reporting, and being instantly monitored, an attack is unlikely to be evident for many minutes, and its source will probably not be pinpointed for hours (if ever). If detectors are not available, an attack will probably not be evident until the first patients appear in large numbers at emergency rooms, more than 24 hours later. During this time, an attacker can readily move to another site, with a prepositioned (or very portable) stockpile of anthrax.

Biological Terror

"I am convinced that biological terror will strike the United States," said Dr. Kenneth Alibek, who developed bioweapons for the Soviet Union before defecting to the west in 1992. Alibek, an anthrax specialist who now works to combat biological weapons, warned the members of a congressional national security subcommittee that we have much to fear from germ warfare. Said a somber Alibek: "Existing defenses against these weapons are dangerously inadequate."

These sentiments were shared on the Senate side by Ted Kennedy, D-Mass., who told his colleagues, "Every day we delay in expanding our capabilities exposes innocent Americans to needless danger. We cannot afford to wait."

Susan Katz Keating, *American Legion*, December 2001.

In sum, biological weapons readily lend themselves not only to catastrophic effects but also to reload. This is a special attribute. Even a terrorist detonation of a nuclear weapon, catastrophic as it would be, is not likely to be repeated quickly.

Campaign Terrorism

Reload is especially important in the context of political terrorism. Some terrorism is expressive. A nihilist, vandal, or lunatic who believes he is initiating an apocalypse may see his act as an end unto itself, a self-contained assertion of his or his god's anger or power. The terrorists of most concern to us act, however, for instrumental reasons. They produce terror as a means to a political end.

Acts of terror may achieve political ends by physical destruction, but they operate primarily in psychological and political dimensions. Instrumental terrorists aim to disable governments by diverting resources, enhancing divisiveness, and undermining the confidence of citizens in their government. Ultimately, if a government cannot protect its citizens, acts of terror sap their targets' will to persevere in policies the terrorists oppose. Viewed this way, terrorists and governments may be thought of as in a competition over whether the safety and morale of the target population can be maintained.

Reload is of enormous importance in this context. Traditional acts of terrorism enjoy climaxes but exhaust themselves and then face the prospect of retaliation. Biological terrorism affords the possibility of repeated attack, undermining confidence and forcing ever-escalating investments of resources to achieve a modicum of defense. If, during a period of recurring biological attack, we are inadequately prepared, then the psychologically and politically corrosive consequences of the attack will be amplified, as our population will ask: why wasn't more done? In the extreme but chillingly plausible case, an unprecedented effect may be achieved: our national power to manage the consequences of repeated biological attacks could be exhausted while the terrorist ability to reload remains intact? . . .

A first step [to better prepare for such attacks] is to recognize the risk of reload and to prepare accordingly. One of the most important questions military commanders are trained to ask when they are under fire is: "Is this the first in a series of attacks?" The answer, gleaned from intelligence, guides the commander's force posture, tactics, and allocation of resources. We have slighted this question in our planning for bioterrorism.

[My recommendation is to] establish planning scenarios and set resource requirements on the assumption that biological weapons will permit terrorists to rapidly "reload" and repeatedly attack. In this light, we must prepare for biological attacks repeated in different American cities rather rapidly after one another. Plan to defend against a campaign, not just an attack.

"*The greatest biological killers occur naturally in the form of emerging and reemerging infections.*"

Natural Epidemics Pose a Greater Threat than Bioterrorism

Hospital Infection Control

People may have more anxieties about bioterrorism, but naturally occurring epidemics pose a greater threat to world health, argue the editors of *Hospital Infection Control* in the following viewpoint. Millions have died from AIDS and various flu pandemics, and reemerging diseases such as West Nile virus and tuberculosis are finding new niches. The ability of microbes to "jump species"—move from infecting animals to infecting humans—and the transmission of viruses through organ transplants and blood transfusion can have catastrophic effects, the authors maintain. *Hospital Infection Control* is a monthly magazine published by American Health Consultants, a health care information provider.

As you read, consider the following questions:

1. How many people died in the flu pandemic of 1918, according to the authors?
2. According to the authors, how many people are likely to die of AIDS in the next twenty years?
3. In the opinion of Anthony Fauci, quoted in this viewpoint, why are diseases like Ebola more of a threat to health care workers than they are to the general population?

Hospital Infection Control, "Nature: The Mother of All Bioterrorism: The Many-Headed Hydra Is Always 'Out There,'" vol. 30, issue 1, January 2003, p. 57. Copyright © 2003 by Thomson Healthcare Company. Reproduced by permission.

While much fear and consternation swirls around the possibilities of bioterrorism, it is wise to remember that the greatest biological killers occur naturally in the form of emerging and reemerging infections.

"The worst bioterrorist can actually be nature itself," said Anthony Fauci, MD, director of the National Institute of Allergy and Infectious Diseases at the National Institutes of Health in Bethesda, MD. Fauci spoke on the subject recently in San Diego at the Interscience Conference on Antimicrobial Agents and Chemotherapy. "A classic, truly emerging disease, HIV, originated in sub-Sahara Africa. A reemerging disease, West Nile virus, landed in the East Coast of the United States and is now permeating our entire country. [There are] multiple different types of antibiotic-resistant tuberculosis, malaria, staphylococcus, enterococcus—all emerging and reemerging diseases. It is a continuing spectrum. Just this past summer [of 2002] we had an extraordinary outbreak in Madagascar of flu with a very, very high case fatality rate. Again, it just reminds us of what's out there."

Bioterrorism Versus Natural Disease

Yet the fear factor is strikingly different between bioterrorism and natural disease, though the patient outcomes may be far worse with the latter. The anthrax attacks [of 2003] disrupted government and instilled widespread fear, but the death toll was five people. Compare that to West Nile virus, which has infected 2,200 people and killed 108 of them since it first appeared in North America in 1999. Endemic in some parts of the world, the virus is a classic example of a reemerging microbe, Fauci noted. Having now reached the West Coast of the United States after first appearing in New York, West Nile virus is digging into new niches and at times causing a "polio-like" syndrome. "[We are seeing] that it is transmitted by organ transplantation and likely by blood transfusion. More recently genetic elements of West Nile were isolated from the breast milk of an infected mother," Fauci said.

The death toll of natural occurring epidemics has been staggering. "The flu pandemic of 1918 killed [more than] 25 million people worldwide, 750,000 in the United States," he said. "HIV/AIDS—60 million people thus far infected, 20 million of whom are dead. The projections are that 45 million more people will be infected in the next 10 years and [there will be] 75 million deaths in the next 20 years." While bioterrorism scenarios remain the prime topic of discussion, the world actually flirted with a huge biological disaster when the avian flu strain HSN1 emerged in Hong Kong a few years ago. Stamped out quickly by public health officials, the unusual strain had the potential to achieve pandemic status.

Cam. © 2003 by Caglecartoons.com. Reproduced by permission of Daryl Cagle for Slate.com.

"The [1918] flu pandemic is a most extraordinary stamp on our history," Fauci said. "Those of us in the field of public health and emerging disease, if there's one thing that we're concerned about, it's the next flu pandemic. That's something that would be naturally occurring if it does occur—hopefully, naturally occurring—but it will be something that could have an impact that totally transcends some of the [bioterrorism] things that we're talking about. We saw little blips of that with the avian flu strain that first emerged in Hong Kong, but that was jumped on by the [Centers for Disease Control and Prevention] and the Chinese authorities in a manner that actually interrupted what potentially could have been a catastrophe."

In addition, diseases of zoonotic origin such as HIV constantly threaten to "jump species" and become an infecting agent in humans. "So it was not surprising that [HIV] happened, but what it resulted in is an enormous pandemic that is ranking among the worst in history."

Ebola and Smallpox

In contrast, natural occurring viral hemorrhagic fevers (e.g., Ebola, Marburg, and Lhasa) are more a threat to health care workers treating victims than the general population, he added. "Although Ebola is a terrible disease, the most vulnerable people are the physicians, nurses, and health care providers who take care of [the infected]—not the people who are out in the community," he said. "Because by the time someone gets to the point of spreading Ebola, they're generally so sick they can't get out of bed. So it's a 'big horror' microbe but not necessarily [a risk] of spreading from person to person." That transmission factor may make Ebola a less likely choice as a bioterror weapon, "but then there are other ways of spreading disease," Fauci warned. The intersection between natural infection and bioterrorism occurs most dramatically with smallpox, an ancient scourge that has been eradicated in nature but lives on as a prospect of war. There are few microbes that rival the impact on civilization as smallpox, which has been identified in DNA analysis on the mummy of the Pharaoh Ramses. In the context of world history; the last few smallpox-free decades are strikingly brief.

"Back as early as the early 1900s, there were a lot of cases in the United States—almost 50,000 cases from 1900 to 1904," he said. "Importantly, the last reported case in the United States was in 1949, and we stopped vaccinating in 1972."

"The real lesson here is not about SARS, but about our capacity to respond to the next big biological threat."

The SARS Epidemic Reveals the Need to Improve Disease Prevention Strategies

Mark Parascandola

In 2002 a new infectious disease emerged: severe acute respiratory syndrome, commonly referred to as SARS. As Mark Parascandola reports in the following viewpoint, public health officials were disturbed to find that SARS had reached epidemic levels in southern China months before the international community learned of the new virus. The illness traveled to several Asian countries, Canada, and the United States, infecting thousands and killing hundreds, and it prompted the World Health Organization to issue a global alert in March 2003. Although the epidemic declined over the next several months, the emergence of an illness like SARS reveals the need for increased international cooperation and surveillance of microbial threats, the author concludes. Parascandola is an epidemiologist for the National Cancer Institute in Bethesda, Maryland.

As you read, consider the following questions:

1. According to Parascandola, to whom was the initial SARS outbreak in Toronto, Canada, eventually traced?
2. What is the death rate for people infected with SARS, according to the author?

Mark Parascandola, "Learning from SARS," *In These Times*, vol. 27, August 11, 2003, pp. 20–21. Copyright © 2003 by *In These Times*. Reproduced by permission.

When the World Health Organization (WHO) issued its first-ever Global Alert on March 12 [2003], declaring Severe Acute Respiratory Syndrome (SARS) to be "a worldwide health threat," the international scientific community mobilized overnight. Within weeks, scientists had identified the coronavirus that causes the disease and mapped the virus' genetic code. Biotech companies jumped at the opportunity to develop diagnostic tests and other weapons for the war against SARS. And some scientists predict that, on the fast track, a vaccine could be completed within three years. But the progress of public health efforts to control the disease have proceeded at a slower, less deliberate pace.

A Dearth of Information

The WHO alert followed reports of 150 suspected cases and several deaths in a one-week period from Hong Kong, Canada, Indonesia, the Philippines, Singapore, Thailand, and Vietnam. Early details were spotty. News coverage described the disease as a "form of pneumonia" or a "superflu." Its origin was uncertain, though attention focused briefly on an American businessman who had traveled from Shanghai to Hanoi and later died of the disease in Hong Kong. Terrorism had not been ruled out as an explanation.

In fact, the epidemic had been festering for months in the southern Chinese province of Guangdong, but obtaining reliable information from the Chinese government proved difficult. When the WHO began releasing daily SARS reports, beginning March 17 [2003], the statistics for China were simply left blank with a footnote explaining that they were being "updated." After a week of waiting in Beijing, WHO investigators were finally given permission to enter Guangdong province in early April. But over the following weeks, journalists recounted stories of patients being hidden from investigators and physicians being instructed not to publicize SARS deaths.

Aided by modern travel, the microbes traversed the globe undetected. On March 5 an elderly woman who had returned home to Toronto after 10 days in Hong Kong died from a chest infection, but not before passing the disease on to her son. By April 23 when the WHO issued a travel advisory for Toronto, 136 cases and 15 deaths had been reported in the province of Ontario. However, because the outbreak could be traced to a single carrier, the Toronto health authorities had a better chance of containing it. They closed infected hospitals and identified contacts of infected individuals, and by May 14 with no new cases in 20 days, Canada was removed from the WHO list of SARS affected areas.

But victory had been declared too soon. Two weeks later, Toronto was back on the WHO watch list with 60 new cases. More than 7,000 people were ordered into 10 days of home quarantine, including an entire suburban Catholic high school. When some kids opted to take their quarantine at local shopping malls, public health officials were quick to remind the public of their authority. Ontario Health Minister Tony Clement warned, "We can chain them to a bed if that's what it takes." (Toronto was removed from the list again on July 12.)

Finger-Pointing

Meanwhile, there was much finger-pointing over who was to blame for the resurgence. Biologically, it was traced to a single "silent SARS case," a 96-year-old patient at North York General Hospital who did not show classic symptoms of the disease and was thought to have died of pneumonia. But some blamed senior medical officials for letting their guard down when the initial outbreak subsided. Hospital workers were told they no longer needed to wear masks and gloves if they were not working with SARS patients. In addition, medical officials assumed that anyone who did not exhibit "classical" symptoms was not a SARS case (a particularly dangerous assumption when dealing with a novel agent).

Some commentators also accused Canadian health officials of practicing their own, more subtle brand of number-fudging. The Ontario Ministry of Health and Long Term Care insisted on using its own medical definition of a "probable" SARS case, which was stricter than the WHO definition because it required evidence that the disease was "progressing" on top of evidence of infection. Only the probable cases go into the official statistical reports, so this maneuver tended to lowball the morbidity count. A cynical observer might believe that this was an intentional strategy designed to stave off another travel ban. Eventually, at the urging of his own public health experts, Clement agreed to use the WHO definition, which had the immediate effect of almost tripling the official number of Canadian cases.

Thinking Strategically

It is time to think more strategically about the future of our nation's public-health system. . . . Because of their impact on society, a coordinated strategy is necessary to understand, detect, control, and ultimately prevent infectious diseases. We believe that far more significant investments in public health will need to occur if we are to prepare the nation's public-health system to protect us from the leading causes of death, prepare us for bioterrorism and chemical terrorism and respond to the public-health crises of the day.

I hope we all recognize that this SARS event is not over, and that we still have a ways to go to ensure containment. In the future, we will always be one plane ride away, one infected person away and one epidemic away from a global tragedy. We cannot lower our guard, not today, not tomorrow.

Georges Benjamin, congressional testimony, May 7, 2003.

In the United States, public health leaders remain puzzled about why there have been so few cases here (73 cases and no deaths in total). "We still do not have a complete understanding of why, so far at least, we've not had it spread into the community," Centers for Disease Control and Prevention Director [CDC] Dr. Julie Gerberding admitted recently. But so far, the best explanation is pure luck. U.S. Health and Human Services Secretary Tommy Thompson added to growing public fears when he suggested that the disease might return with greater force in the fall flu season. "I am not confident at all," he said. "I do not think SARS is going to go away."

Currently, the risk to individuals in the United States and Canada remains extremely low. Yet there is little specific advice that government officials can offer individuals for protecting themselves. When it came to giving advice to the public, Gerberding simply said: "My advice is to kind of follow the same rules your mother taught you in kindergarten.

Keep your hands clean, and cover your mouth with a tissue if you're coughing and sneezing."

A Turning Point

According to the most recent reports, a turning point has been reached, and the epidemic appears to be in decline worldwide. As of July 2 [2003], the WHO reported a total of 8,442 cases and 812 deaths from SARS since the disease first became known. But there have been fewer new cases appearing in recent weeks. Additionally, the Chinese government has taken a more vigorous and open approach to combating the epidemic, setting up roadblocks and even (against the advice of public health officials worldwide) warning that individuals who violate their quarantine could be sentenced to death.

Why should SARS warrant such global attention? After all, there are far more deadly diseases out there. WHO officials argue that the intense focus on SARS is warranted for now because there is a limited window of opportunity within which to defeat the disease. David Heymann, WHO executive director for communicable diseases, explained, "When we put out the announcement about this new disease, one of our major concerns was that maybe we could stop this disease from becoming endemic."

Moreover, while the number of deaths has been relatively small so far, that could change dramatically if the disease were to spread freely throughout Asia. Estimates of the death rate for people infected with the SARS virus run from 4 percent to 10 percent. The death rate from the Spanish Flu, which circled the globe and killed 50 million people between 1918 and 1920, was lower, about 3 percent. But what made the Spanish Flu so deadly was not a high mortality rate, but the fact that it was so easily transmitted and infected entire populations. In public health terms, the probability of death for the infected individual is only one part of the equation.

The Lesson of SARS

The SARS epidemic has also forced discussion about public health legal authority. When a woman arrived in the United

States on a plane from China with a fever and cough, CDC officials at the airport wanted her taken to the hospital for examination. However, when she refused to comply, they were powerless to do anything. Federal law allows for the "apprehension, detention, or conditional release of individuals" for quarantine purposes, but only for diseases that are specified in the federal regulations, including cholera, plague, smallpox, and other ancient scourges. On April 4 [2003], President [George W.] Bush issued an Executive Order adding SARS to the list.

Public health experts warn that the real lesson here is not about SARS, but about our capacity to respond to the next big biological threat. In other words, disease prevention requires more than strengthening our own borders. It requires training experts in epidemiology and surveillance and establishing state-of-the-art laboratories around the globe. If SARS persists in Asia for the long term, it will continue to threaten us. As Barry Bloom, dean of the Harvard School of Public Health, writes in a recent issue of *Science.* "In a world that is increasingly angry at the United States, the lesson here is that it is time to support a global war on disease."

"Overreaction is a threat whenever governments face an apparent crisis."

The SARS Epidemic Reveals the Dangers of Overreaction to Disease

Declan McCullagh

Civil liberties, health, and reason are endangered when governments overreact to the threat of communicable diseases, contends Declan McCullagh in the following viewpoint. During the SARS outbreak of 2002, for example, China initially denied the existence of the illness, enabling the epidemic to spread. By May of 2003 China had isolated its SARS carriers and declared that anyone who broke quarantine would be executed. In the United States, McCullagh reports, several states passed laws enabling governors to seize assets, forcibly vaccinate and quarantine, and declare a state of emergency after an outbreak of SARS or other infectious diseases. Such state laws may lead to government abuses, the author warns. McCullagh is the Washington correspondent for News.com.

As you read, consider the following questions:

1. How did mixed signals from state governments affect the outcome of the 1918 flu epidemic in the United States, according to McCullagh?
2. What is the Model Emergency Health Powers Act, according to the author?
3. How did panic mongers take advantage of public anxiety during the 2003 SARS outbreak, according to McCullagh?

Visiting Singapore is a little like flying into some twisted *Father Knows Best* time warp. Lining the streets next to such familiar stores as Reebok, Esprit, and Timberland are government ministries with names like "Board of Film Censors," along with buildings housing the "Social Development Unit" state-run dating service and the "Home Ownership for the People Scheme."

For a few weeks in April and May [2003], such downtown streets were speckled with gauzy white squares: mask-wearing Singaporeans fearful of catching the deadly SARS pneumonia. They had reason to be concerned. According to the World Health Organization [WHO] Sudden Acute Respiratory Syndrome kills roughly 15 to 20 percent of the people who contract it, and it had been spreading through parts of Asia faster than pirated copies of the latest Microsoft beta release. What's more, the average death rate can be misleading. SARS is an age-sensitive disease: If you're over 65 years old and you have the misfortune of being infected, the WHO believes your death-rate odds are a dismaying 50 percent or higher.

Singapore's nanny-state meddling and unabashed authoritarianism may have spared it the worst. Even though it had the third-worst outbreak of SARS, behind China and Hong Kong, Singapore's death rate was 15 percent, lower than the less severe North America outbreak centered in Toronto. (Canada's death rate, as of press time, was 17.5 percent.) . . .

When SARS hit, the authoritarian proclivities of Singapore's government were channeled into aggressive quarantines. After a few possible SARS cases were identified at the popular Pasir Panjang Wholesale Market, the state took no chances. Nearly 2,000 people who had worked at the market between April 5 and April 19 were placed under mandatory home quarantine for 10 days. Health Minister Lim Hng Kiang said a team of 50 to 60 nurses would make house calls on quarantined homes, and the government would offer a daily home quarantine allowance of $41. Web cams were installed in quarantined homes for surveillance, with residents asked to step in front of the camera on demand. Anyone nabbed for flouting the quarantine was outfitted with an electronic tracking bracelet.

Medical Powers

The good news—for now—is that SARS is less of a threat than it was [in the spring of 2003], though it could return with a vengeance when winter comes to the northern hemisphere and people spend more time inside in close quarters. As of this writing there have been no confirmed SARS deaths in the U.S., and an analysis prepared by *The New England Journal of Medicine* indicates that the worldwide SARS growth rate is more arithmetic than exponential.

But if the virus does return, other nations besides Singapore will have to balance suggestions such as broad quarantine orders with the preservation of civil liberties and the rights to privacy, property, and freedom of movement.

What does this mean for the U.S.? What might happen is anyone's guess, but imagine if there were a serious outbreak [in the] fall that threatened to overwhelm the nation's health system. This is the kind of scenario the Centers for Disease Control and Prevention (CDC) dreads—one in which hospitals are deluged with scores or hundreds of patients showing up at the same time. As physicians in Singapore and Hong Kong found out, emergency rooms and critical care wards can be lethally efficient in spreading SARS. Government officials at the state and federal level have been warning since [the September 11, 2001, terrorist attacks] that the U.S. is not prepared for a biological attack. SARS appears to be natural in origin, but the effects could be the same.

A Cautionary Tale

So consider, as a thought experiment, what might happen in the U.S. after a major outbreak of SARS or a similar communicable disease.

We already know that President George W. Bush has signed an executive order triggering a World War I–era law that lets him add SARS to the ranks of such diseases as cholera, smallpox, and the plague. The current version of that law grew out of well-justified fears of the deadly flu epidemic of 1918, sometimes called Spanish influenza, which infected about 28 percent of all Americans and killed about 675,000— about 10 times the number of U.S. soldiers felled in battle during the war. Globally, over 30 million people died, and even President Woodrow Wilson was infected in early 1919 while negotiating the Treaty of Versailles.

Reactions to the 1918 epidemic provide a cautionary tale. State governments across the U.S. responded by levying quarantines and imposing mask laws. In San Francisco, the city sterilized public telephones and drinking fountains. It also required people to wear gauze masks in all public places, giving rise to the far-too-optimistic slogan: "Wear a Mask and Save Your Life! A Mask is 99% Proof Against Influenza." In November, city sirens wailed to signal that it was safe to remove the masks—an announcement that was terribly premature, as thousands more people came down with influenza the following month.

In Philadelphia, city officials made the fatal mistake of sending mixed signals. While one agency was warning against public coughing, sneezing, and spitting, the Department of Health and Charities was informing the public that influenza would not spread outside the military. Then, over a matter of weeks, nearly 13,000 people died. Too late, the city government ordered schools, churches, theaters, and other public gathering places closed. Elsewhere, "openfaced sneezers" were fined and the District of Columbia imposed blanket quarantines that restricted residents to their homes. . . .

Difficult Trade-Offs

And today? Under current federal law, 42 U.S.C. 264, the Surgeon General has broad power to "make and enforce" any rules that may be necessary to prevent the spread of communicable diseases. The law makes for fascinating—if disquieting—reading.

It gives federal officials the authority to appoint quarantine officers, establish quarantine stations, and detain Americans "reasonably believed to be infected" with a communicable disease. Anyone violating a quarantine order can be punished by a fine of up to $1,000 and a one-year prison term. The law applies only to a list of deadly and easily communicable diseases that the president may amend at will, which Bush did in his executive order that added SARS to the list.

Then there's MEHPA, the proposed Model Emergency Health Powers Act, which began appearing in state capitals soon after the anthrax scare of late 2001. It expands upon the emergency authority that many cities and states already have arrogated themselves for times of crisis, making explicit what powers public health officials will have.

Among them: seizing property and land as "necessary to respond to the public health emergency," forcibly vaccinating Americans against infectious diseases, and quarantining those who refuse. No court order is necessary to detain someone: "The public health authority may temporarily isolate or quarantine an individual or groups of individuals through a written directive." Backing the proposal are the CDC, the National Governors Association, the National Conference of State Legislatures, and the National Association of County and City Health Officials. So far about two dozen states have enacted MEHPA into law.

Folk Remedies and Firecrackers

Like other dread diseases, SARS has already ignited a flurry of hoaxes and folk remedies to ward off infection. In remote areas of China, people have set off firecrackers to fend off infection, and markets abound with herbs and roots said to confer immunity from SARS.

In the United States, the Food and Drug Administration (FDA) has warned at least eight individuals to halt false advertising for remedies they claim will protect against SARS. "We've been going after people who are out there touting all kinds of fraudulent products as protection from SARS," says Murray Lumpkin, the FDA's principal associate commissioner. "Their claims are totally unsubstantiated. It's nothing less than health fraud."

Mary H. Cooper, *CQ Researcher*, June 20, 2003.

MEHPA highlights the difficult trade-offs of balancing individual liberty with community security. While it is a serious step to limit a person's freedom of movement, there seems to be little alternative in the case of highly infectious communicable diseases. The question then becomes how the law should be worded and how it might work in practice. Critics warn that earlier versions of MEHPA would have handed governors the power to declare public health emergencies over tobacco smoke or obesity—and seize an extremely dangerous amount of power in the process. The liberal American Civil Liberties Union and the conservative Free Congress Foundation and American Legislative Exchange Council joined to oppose it.

According to the ACLU, MEHPA permits a governor to "declare a state of emergency unilaterally and without judicial oversight, fails to provide modern due process procedures for quarantine and other emergency powers, it lacks adequate compensation for seizure of assets, and contains no checks on the power to order forced treatment and vaccination."

Such powers can be used carefully and can be wildly abused; it's far too early to make predictions. Yet it's worth remembering—and the 1918 flu epidemic is a major re- minder—that government officials are as prone to mistakes as anyone else. Guénael Rodier, the World Health Organi- zation's director of communicable disease and response, re- cently admitted that the organization could have done a much better job of responding to SARS early [in 2003] by making an earlier public warning. If that had happened, "Toronto would very likely have been spared a SARS out- break on the scale it has worked so admirably to contain," Rodier wrote in a commentary for the *Canadian Medical As- sociation Journal*. Richard Schabas, a former minister of health for Ontario, has accused provincial officials of not an- alyzing SARS data properly, and causing unnecessary panic by overreacting when the disease was confined to hospitals.

Panic and Other Responses

That's hindsight, of course. But overreaction is a threat whenever governments face an apparent crisis. Officials may respond to pressure either because they believe the crisis is genuine or because they think the appearance of activity on their part is necessary to head off panic. Who wants to re- peat what Toronto experienced, when the WHO drove a stiletto through the heart of tourist travel by effectively declaring it a SARS hot zone?

Take what happened in 1998 and 1999, during the so- called Y2K [year 2000] computer glitch. Canadian newspa- pers reported at the time that the government was consider- ing martial law and the invocation of the Emergencies Act in response to Y2K disruptions. In the U.S., Sen. Robert Bennett (R-Utah) asked the Pentagon what plans it has "in the event of a Y2K-induced breakdown of community services that might call for martial law"; a House subcommittee recommended that then-President [Bill] Clinton consider declaring a Y2K "national emergency."

One traditional way to manage public reaction is to manage tightly the flow of information, a task that technological advance has made more difficult. Reports of the spread of SARS, for instance, rocketed around the globe even faster than the virus itself. During the early days of the outbreak, an intensive-care specialist at a hospital in Hong Kong turned to e-mail lists to distribute his stark, first-hand reports. "This pneumonia is out there in the community," Tom Buckley told the Critical Care Medicine mailing list on March 24 [2003], in a widely forwarded message. "The numbers are increasing daily, and a third hospital is being prepared for the influx. How big this is going to get is anyone's guess." Buckley warned that the Hong Kong government "is downplaying the whole thing presumably because of the economic implications." Buckley's post was prescient. In the two months following his warning, cases of SARS in Hong Kong leapt sevenfold, from 260 to over 1,700 infections. (When contacted for a response, Hong Kong's Health, Welfare and Food bureau replied with a statement saying: "To reassure you that we are not trying to downplay any of the effects, we recognize that in fact the public health considerations must be first and foremost and all the other things are secondary to this.")

Deception and Misinformation

In China, the birthplace of SARS, the communist government lied for months. Beijing officially, and implausibly, denied the existence of hundreds of SARS patients in hospitals that had been visited by Western journalists. Then China Premier Wen Jiabao took the unusual step of saying that while progress had been made in limiting the spread of SARS, "the overall situation remains grave." This is the same government that [in 2002], in just one day, upped its official estimate of HIV infections from 30,000 cases to 1 million. In a sign of China's growing desperation, the government said in May [2003] that those who break quarantine and spread SARS would be executed. If authoritarianism helped save lives in Singapore, in China it has been deadly.

In this climate of official deception, misinformation about SARS has been spreading so efficiently it would do the common cold proud. Some residents of China's Shanxi province reportedly place their faith in steamed vinegar. A Singapore department store advertises perfume atomizers as effective SARS countermeasures. A teenager's Web hoax claiming Hong Kong's borders would be closed prompted runs on canned foods and toilet paper. A supermarket owner in Sacramento spent two weeks arguing that, contrary to rumors, neither he nor his family is infected with SARS and his stores are entirely safe. A Sacramento city councilman tried to quell panic by bravely chewing a ceremonial Granny Smith apple from the store's produce section in front of reporters.

An in-depth *New York Times* analysis showed that America is not immune to this 21st-century information contagion. The *Times* reported that high levels of anxiety existed in states such as New York, California, and Washington that experienced the most SARS cases or had sizeable Asian-American communities. New York City Mayor Michael Bloomberg was worried enough about public panic to dine in a Chinatown restaurant and then hold a press conference about it. OnlineAllergy Relief.com, an Internet retailer in Metairie, Louisiana, that sells air filters and purification products, reports that business is booming. "We have gone through case after case of masks," a representative says. "They're just slow to come in now. . . . A lot of things are back ordered. Our manufacturer doesn't have a really big supply."

Anxiety Versus Technology

Panic mongers inevitably arise to prey on public nervousness. Web sites of dubious provenance tout dietary supplements—colloidal silver, oregano oil—as effective anti-SARS measures. Spam touting SARS remedies is on the rise. Gary North, the Christian Reconstructionist who has made a living predicting that modern society will end in panic and ruin, has seized on SARS. In 1980, North forecast rationing of housing and a nuclear war with the Soviet Union, warning his followers to buy "gold, silver, a safe place outside the major cities." Later he found rich topics in AIDS and then Y2K, recommending to his newsletter subscribers that they head for the hills to avoid total social collapse. In an announcement in April [2003], North seized on SARS. He wrote: "It's a race between medical science and the bugs. There is no scientific reason to believe that the scientists will always beat the bugs."

Perhaps not. While technology may aid panic-mongering, technological advance is also what makes the fight against SARS so different from previous epidemics. Technology lets researchers collaborate in ways simply not possible just a few years ago. Perhaps the most impressive way in which research has been accelerated is in the analysis of the virus' complete genetic code. More than a dozen sequences of the virus—all demonstrating slight differences, which is typical for a coronavirus—are up on the WHO's Web site. As a result of this genetic sequencing and collaboration, companies like AVI BioPharma in Oregon think that the first drug to combat SARS could be available in months, not years. . . .

Nearly 100 years ago, the Spanish Flu tested medical science's ability to respond to a deadly worldwide threat, with researchers in 1918 venturing beyond the germ theory of disease and postulating the then-novel existence of a virus as the cause of the infection. Their attempts to unravel the mystery of influenza soon led to the creation of a hybrid vaccine administered to the British military.

Today, researchers already have used the virus' genetic sequence to create tests that weed out people who may have breathing problems but are not infected with SARS. While the panic mongers have an undeniable head start, so far the ability of modern science to deal with such a novel and destructive threat seems up to the task. Let's only hope that governments' reactions to SARS are equally careful.

"The AIDS epidemic has become a mounting global tragedy with 20 million killed and 40 million infected."

The AIDS Epidemic Is a Serious Global Threat

Ed Susman

Acquired immunodeficiency syndrome (AIDS) threatens nations across the world, writes Ed Susman in the following viewpoint. Globally, about 40 million people are living with AIDS or with the human immunodeficiency virus (HIV), which is primarily spread through sexual contact, unsafe needle injections, and tainted blood products. AIDS has had its most devastating impact in the nations of sub-Saharan Africa and in the Caribbean, where poverty, misinformation, and government inaction have contributed to the spread of the epidemic, Susman reports. In many developed nations, moreover, new HIV diagnoses are on the rise among injecting drug users, sex workers, and gay and bisexual men. Susman, a freelance writer, is a regular contributor to United Press International.

As you read, consider the following questions:
1. How many South Africans are infected with HIV, according to Susman?
2. How has Cuba controlled the spread of HIV among its population, according to the author?
3. In the city of Togliatti, Russia, what percentage of injecting drug users are HIV positive, according to Susman?

Ed Susman, "The Global Face of AIDS," *World & I*, vol. 19, March 2004, pp. 140–47.

Sometime early in the twentieth century, possibly preceding the Great Depression, a virus carried by African primates jumped from one species to another, becoming HIV (human immunodeficiency virus). Fifty years later, on continents far from sub-Saharan Africa, HIV was discovered and identified as the cause of AIDS (autoimmune deficiency syndrome).

The AIDS epidemic has become a mounting global tragedy with 20 million killed and 40 million infected. Worldwide in 2003, according to estimates from the Joint United Nations Programme on HIV/AIDS (UNAIDS), roughly five million people were infected with HIV. More than three million are expected to die from complications of the disease in 2004.

In Africa, the pandemic's effects are unmatched in their severity and tragic consequences. About 29.6 million of these infected with or dying of HIV/AIDS live in sub-Saharan Africa, where the virus spread to 3.2 million more people in 2003 alone and 58 percent of those living with HIV are women. Although the horror and extent of the disease on the African continent have brought promises of assistance from world leaders, including President George W. Bush, a combination of poverty, government inaction, myth, and stigma continues to drive the epidemic to levels that are difficult for citizens of the developed countries to comprehend.

Highly opportunistic and robust, HIV thrives and spreads among humans primarily because of promiscuous sexual behavior, unsafe medical injections, needle sharing among users of addictive drugs, mother to child transmission, and, in some parts of the world, tainted blood products. For this article, however, the focus is not on the behaviors but on the national-level consequences and responses in six regions of the world: Africa, Asia, the Caribbean and Latin America, eastern Europe, western Europe, and the United States.

Africa

In Africa, where 16 nations have disease prevalence rates that exceed 10 percent—20 times the 0.5 percent HIV incidence rate in the United States and western Europe—many governments have ignored the epidemic that fills hospital wards and leaves millions of homeless orphans in its wake.

Nearly five million South Africans—15 percent of the population—are infected with HIV. Nevertheless, the government has for more than three years blocked efforts to provide pregnant women with drugs that can prevent transmission of HIV to their babies. It now promises that treatment programs will be in place by 2005.

It is estimated that 8,000 babies are born to HIV-infected mothers each month in South Africa. Without treatment, 33 to 40 percent of those infants will have HIV. With treatment, less than 2 percent would be born with HIV, which kills most infected babies before they are four years old.

An estimated 600 people die from AIDS every day in South Africa, and thousands more die in Botswana, Swaziland, Zimbabwe, Malawi, and all across Africa. Only in a few places are drugs being distributed; only in a few countries are preventive messages being heeded.

The Human Impact

Though these numbers are grim, the human impact behind them is numbing. As Dr. Thomas Quinn, professor of medicine at Johns Hopkins University in Baltimore, explained: "One has to consider Africa's main agricultural society. Seven million farmers have died due to AIDS. One has to ask who is farming the land.

"There is also the educational process as well as the working process," he said. "Eighty-five percent of teacher deaths in the last 20 years have been due to AIDS.

"In fact, AIDS is the leading cause of death within the continent. Because it affects many people in their young, reproductive ages, we are left with a very large number of orphans. These children are not necessarily infected with HIV but are left behind due to the premature death of their parents.

"From the global perspective the HIV epidemic has reversed many of the developmental gains that have been achieved in many areas of the world, particularly those made over the last three decades," said Quinn. "There has been an economic decline, particularly on the African continent, with estimates of that decline ranging from 10 to 40 percent—a staggering figure in an area that is already economically fragile.

"One result is health-system chaos. In some places, 50 to 70 or 80 percent of hospital beds may be occupied by HIV-infected people with opportunistic infections, many of which go untreated. All of this results in a spiraling factor of political instability," Quinn noted.

"Africa is where AIDS has entrenched itself in the last two to three decades and is still spiraling out of control. The spread of HIV continues relentlessly across the continent."

On a more positive note, he observed that some countries are making a difference in limiting its spread and in treating HIV-infected patients. Uganda, for example, has successfully reduced the incidence and prevalence of HIV through behavioral education programs, and Botswana and Senegal are implementing effective treatment programs.

Asia

While Africa's social, economic, and humanitarian catastrophe has caught the world's attention, a pending AIDS disaster in Asia barely causes a blip on the radar screen.

Officials are aware of the disease's growing incidence in India and China, which are home to more than 2 billion people. They have sounded alarms, but in vulnerable, undereducated, and poverty-stricken areas, those warnings may go unheard.

Consider India. Officially, just under 4 million people are living with HIV infection in the world's most populous democracy, but many doctors in the field think this figure is underestimated.

UNAIDS reports some progress: "New behavioral studies in India suggest that prevention efforts directed at specific populations such as female sex workers and injecting drug users are paying dividends in some states, in the form of higher HIV/AIDS knowledge and condom use.

"However," it reports, "HIV prevalence among those key groups continues to increase in some states, underlining the need for well-planned and sustained interventions on a large scale."

In neighboring Bangladesh, a nation the size of Wisconsin but with a population of 140 million, officially only a few hundred people have HIV infection, said Dr. A.Q.M. Serajul Islam, professor of dermatology and sexually transmitted diseases at Chittagong Medical College and Hospital.

"We screened 400 men at our clinic," he said, "and two of those men were positive for HIV." While that would indicate an infection rate of 0.5 percent at the clinic, Islam was more disturbed by the reactions of his patients.

"They are both married" he said, "but neither of them wanted to have his wife tested. Neither of them even wanted his wife to know that he had HIV." He said that women in Bangladesh seldom receive standard health care and rarely would receive testing for any sexually transmitted disease, let alone AIDS.

In China, which has a population of 1.3 billion, HIV infection is spreading rapidly—especially among injecting drug users. Infected blood products also are contributing to the spread of the disease there.

"The epidemic in China shows no signs of abating," the UNAIDS report stated. "Official estimates put the number of people living with HIV in China at 1 million in mid-2002. Unless effective responses rapidly take hold, a total of 10 million Chinese will have acquired HIV by the end of the decade." To put it another way, 10 million people is equivalent to the entire population of Belgium.

The Caribbean and Latin America

Although AIDS was recognized and identified in the United States and Europe in the 1980s, the extent of the disease throughout the Caribbean and Latin America is still underappreciated. According to UNAIDS: "In several Caribbean countries, adult HIV prevalence rates are surpassed only by the rates experienced in sub-Saharan Africa—making this the second-most affected region in the world."

"I don't think that the situation in Latin America and the Caribbean will ever come close to Africa, where infection rates among adults exceed 10, 15, or 20 percent. But there are already a number of countries in Latin America that have infection rates that exceed 1 percent—and that really is troublesome," said Dr. Richard Keenlyside of the Centers for Disease Control and Prevention [CDC] in Atlanta.

Reports show that the HIV infection rate is higher than 1

percent in 12 countries in the region. This might not seem very high, but at that level the disease already affects overall life expectancy and economic development.

Among the nations that have prevalence rates above 1 percent are impoverished Haiti at 6 percent and the Bahamas at 3.5 percent. Throughout the region, 1.9 million people—nearly half a million in the Caribbean—are infected with HIV.

The Human Consequences of AIDS

The human consequences of AIDS are appalling. In several African countries, most young people will probably die of the disease, often after much suffering, and often in the knowledge that their loved ones will soon die, too. Graveyards are expanding in all directions, and tombs are overrun with weeds because the living are too weak to tend them. The disease aggravates Africa's famines. Hunger and AIDS separately reduce the body's defences against disease, but the two curses reinforce each other. Hungry, immuno-compromised people fall sick, and sick people are often too weak to grow enough food.

Economist, January 17, 2004.

"We are also concerned about the rising epidemic in Guyana," said Keenlyside. The small nation on South America's Caribbean shore has an HIV prevalence rate of 2.7 percent among adults between the ages of 15 and 49.

Keenlyside, associate director for external relations and public health practice for the CDC's Global AIDS Program, said he is encouraged by work being done in the Bahamas, Barbados, and Brazil.

A regional anomaly is Cuba, with an AIDS prevalence rate only one-tenth that of the United States. Cuba controls HIV spread with compulsory HIV education, generic antiretroviral drugs, and universal, mandatory testing, but Keenlyside doubts that such strict methods could be copied in democratic nations.

Eastern Europe

As knowledge of how to control the AIDS epidemic improves, hopes are raised that its spread will be checked. Eastern Europe is one place where those hopes are illusory, as there is a great chasm between knowledge and the political will to act.

Dr. Scott Hammer, professor of infectious diseases at Columbia University, bit his lip and thought about how to describe the AIDS epidemic in eastern Europe. "Explosive," he said, "Explosive."

In countries such as Belarus, Ukraine, Russia, and Uzbekistan, the epidemic is roaring through populations of injecting drug users and is evident among people with other sexually transmitted diseases. In the region, 1.2 million people are infected with HIV.

The 28 states that make up eastern Europe are strapped for cash to run prevention campaigns and treatment programs. More tragically, the governments of the region have generally avoided learning anything from the mistakes made in the West and Africa, where the epidemic is more mature. Dr. Peter Piot, executive director of UNAIDS, singled out Russia for specific criticism, saying the nation expends few resources in fighting the epidemic and does not even have a high-ranking official in charge of those meager efforts.

That is in light of shocking epidemics such as the one in industrial Togliatti, a city with a population of about 750,000, located on the Volga River about 700 miles south of Moscow. Among injecting drug users in that city, about 56 percent were HIV infected, said Ali Judd, a researcher at the Imperial College Faculty of Medicine in London. The year before, 41 percent of those subjects had been HIV negative. More ominous, 43 percent of the drug users surveyed were sex workers.

"We know from past experience," said Hammer, "that once HIV is in the injecting drug population and among sex workers, the virus most likely is already widespread." Outbreaks such as the one in Togliatti are occurring throughout the region, said Dr. Alex Wodak, director of the alcohol and drug treatment service at St. Vincent's Hospital, Sydney, Australia.

Western Europe

While the situation in eastern Europe is worrisome, the wealthier states of western Europe have their own problems with the epidemic. Up to 10 percent of people infected with HIV have a mutated virus that is resistant to at least one class of drugs used to treat the disease.

"Transmission of resistant virus occurs," said Dr. David van de Vijver, an epidemiologist at the University Medical Center in Utrecht, the Netherlands. The pan-European survey looked at rates of drug-resistant virus from 17 countries. In western Europe, an estimated 570,000 people are living with HIV/AIDS.

While most of those countries have stable rates of overall infection, there are still pockets of alarming increases in new infection rates, notably in cities in Portugal and Italy. "We were used to thinking that the epidemic in western Europe was stable," said Lucas Wiessing, a researcher with the European Monitoring Centre for Drugs and Drug Addiction in Lisbon. "But we have found that despite prevention measures, HIV transmission continues at high rates among subgroups of injecting drug users in some countries."

"The situation in Portugal is very scary," said van de Vijver.

The United States

Even in the United States, government agencies are expressing concerns that the "stable" epidemic is showing signs of instability. In this country, 900,000 people are infected with HIV; 180,000 of these are women, 10,000 are children under the age of 15, and there are hints that infection rates are on the rise again. According to Dr. Harold Jaffe, director of the CDC's National Center for HIV, Sexually Transmitted Disease, and Tuberculosis, an increasing number of new HIV infections are being diagnosed among gay and bisexual men. From 2001 to 2002, the number of new HIV diagnoses per year rose 7.1 percent among that population; in the three years from 1999 to 2002, the number of new HIV diagnoses per year has increased by 17.7 percent.

"The AIDS epidemic in the United States is far from over," said Jaffe. "While effective treatments are crucial in our fight against HIV, preventing infection in the first place is still the only true protection against the serious and fatal consequences of this disease."

A World at Risk

Undoubtedly, a few rays of sunshine may pierce the darkness of the HIV/AIDS pandemic, especially in the wealthier nations. For the majority of the 40 million people now infected, however—and the millions more who will become infected with the killer disease this year and next—the sunshine eludes them. Instead, the shadow of a disease that robs people of their most productive years and extends over families, communities, and nations spreads relentlessly across the landscape.

"The AIDS establishment . . . is extremely skilled at 'the manipulation of fear for advancement in terms of money and power.'"

The Extent of the AIDS Epidemic Has Been Exaggerated

Rian Malan

In the following viewpoint Rian Malan contends that faulty computer-generated estimates have greatly exaggerated the impact of the AIDS epidemic. Moreover, he argues, international health organizations and AIDS activists have deliberately used inflated statistics to generate funding to fight the disease. Although Malan grants that AIDS is a serious problem in Africa, he maintains that illnesses such as malaria, tuberculosis, and dysentery are neglected while AIDS receives a disproportionate amount of funding and research. Malan is a writer and journalist in South Africa.

As you read, consider the following questions:
1. According to Malan, what is Epimodel?
2. Why have Africa's schoolteachers been defined as a high-risk HIV group, in the author's opinion?
3. How many Africans get malaria every year, according to Malan?

It was the eve of AIDS Day here [in Cape Town, South Africa]. Rock stars like Bono and Bob Geldof were jetting in for a fundraising concert with Nelson Mandela, and the airwaves were full of dark talk about megadeath and the armies of feral orphans who would surely ransack South Africa's cities in 2017 unless funds were made available to take care of them. My neighbour came up the garden path with a press cutting. 'Read this,' said Capt. David Price, ex-Royal Air Force flyboy. 'Bloody awful.'

It was an article from *The Spectator* describing the bizarre sex practices that contribute to HIV's rampage across the continent. 'One in five of us here in Zambia is HIV positive,' said the report. 'In 1993 our neighbour Botswana had an estimated population of 1.4 million. Today that figure is under a million and heading downwards. Doom merchants predict that Botswana may soon become the first nation in modern times literally to die out. This is AIDS in Africa.'

Really? Botswana has just concluded a census that shows population growing at about 2.7 per cent a year, in spite of what is usually described as the worst AIDS problem on the planet. Total population has risen to 1.7 million in just a decade. If anything, Botswana is experiencing a minor population explosion.

Bad News?

There is similar bad news to the doomsayers in Tanzania's new census, which shows population growing at 2.9 per cent a year. Professional pessimists will be particularly discomforted by developments in the swamplands west of Lake Victoria, where HIV first emerged, and where the depopulated villages of popular mythology are supposedly located. Here, in the district of Kagera, population grew at 2.7 per cent a year before 1988, only to accelerate to 3.1 per cent even as the AIDS epidemic was supposedly peaking. Uganda's latest census tells a broadly similar story, as does South Africa's.

Some might think it good news that the impact of AIDS is less devastating than most laymen imagine, but they are wrong. In Africa, the only good news about AIDS is bad news, and anyone who tells you otherwise is branded a moral leper, bent on sowing confusion and derailing 100,000 worthy fundraising drives. I know this, because several years ago I acquired what was generally regarded as a leprous obsession with the dumbfounding AIDS numbers in my daily papers. They told me that AIDS had claimed 250,000 South African lives in 1999, and I kept saying, this can't possibly be true. What followed was very ugly—ruined dinner parties, broken friendships, ridicule from those who knew better, bitter fights with my wife. After a year or so, she put her foot down. Choose, she said. AIDS or me. So I dropped the subject, put my papers in the garage, and kept my mouth shut.

Reliable Diagnoses?

I cannot understand how any doctor can confidently say that HIV testing in Africa is acceptably reliable. In the developed world HIV testing consists of the Enzyme-Linked Immuno-Sorbent Assay (ELISA) test followed by the Western Blot test. This is because studies have shown that the ELISA test alone produces at least an 83% false positive test result rate. However, in Africa, due to lack of resources, testing usually consists of the ELISA test only. Often, HIV testing is not even performed and people are diagnosed on the basis of unspecific symptoms such as weight loss and diarrhoea.

Mukai Chimutengwende-Gordon, *New African*, November 2002.

As I write, madam is standing behind me with hands on hips, hugely irked by this reversion to bad habits. But looking around, it seems to me that AIDS fever is nearing the danger level, and that some calming thoughts are called for. Bear with me while I explain.

Statistics as Weapons

We all know, thanks to Mark Twain, that statistics are often the lowest form of lie, but when it comes to HIV/AIDS, we suspend all scepticism. Why? AIDS is the most political disease ever. We have been fighting about it since the day it was identified. The key battleground is public perception, and the most deadly weapon is the estimate. When the virus first emerged, I was living in America, where HIV incidence was estimated to be doubling every year or so. Every time I turned on the TV, Madonna popped up to warn me that

'AIDS is an equal-opportunity killer', poised to break out of the drug and gay subcultures and slaughter heterosexuals. In 1985, a science journal estimated that 1.7 million Americans were already infected, with 'three to five million' soon likely to follow suit. Oprah Winfrey told the nation that by 1990 'one in five heterosexuals will be dead of AIDS'.

We now know that these estimates were vastly and indeed deliberately exaggerated, but they achieved the desired end: AIDS was catapulted to the top of the West's spending agenda, and the estimators turned their attention elsewhere. India's epidemic was likened to 'a volcano waiting to explode'. Africa faced 'a tidal wave of death'. By 1992 they were estimating that 'AIDS could clear the whole planet'.

Epimodel

Who were they, these estimators? For the most part, they worked in Geneva for WHO [World Health Organization] or UNAIDS [a United Nations AIDS Organization], using a computer simulator called Epimodel. Every year, all over Africa, blood would be taken from a small sample of pregnant women and screened for signs of HIV infection. The results would be programmed into Epimodel, which transmuted them into estimates. If so many women were infected, it followed that a similar proportion of their husbands and lovers must be infected, too. These numbers would be extrapolated out into the general population, enabling the computer modellers to arrive at seemingly precise tallies of the doomed, the dying and the orphans left behind.

Because Africa is disorganised and, in some parts, unknowable, we had little choice other than to accept these projections. ('We' always expect the worst of Africa anyway.) Reporting on AIDS in Africa became a quest for anecdotes to support Geneva's estimates, and the estimates grew ever more terrible: 9.6 million cumulative AIDS deaths by 1997, rising to 17 million three years later.

Or so we were told. When I visited the worst affected parts of Tanzania and Uganda in 2001, I was overwhelmed with stories about the horrors of what locals called 'Slims', but statistical corroboration was hard to come by. According to government census bureaux, death rates in these areas had been in decline since the second world war. AIDS-era mortality studies yielded some of the lowest overall death rates ever measured. Populations seemed to have exploded even as the epidemic was peaking.

Ask AIDS experts about this, and they say, this is Africa, chaos reigns, the historical data is too uncertain to make valid comparisons. But these same experts will tell you that South Africa is vastly different: 'The only country in sub-Saharan Africa where sufficient deaths are routinely registered to attempt to produce national estimates of mortality,' says Professor Ian Timaeus of the London School of Hygiene and Tropical Medicine. According to Timaeus, upwards of 80 per cent of deaths are registered here, which makes us unique: the only corner of Africa where it is possible to judge computer-generated AIDS estimates against objective reality.

Odd Numbers

In the year 2000, Timaeus joined a team of South African researchers bent on eliminating all doubts about the magnitude of AIDS' impact on South African mortality. Sponsored by the Medical Research Council [MRC], the team's mission was to validate (for the first time ever) the output of AIDS computer models against actual death registration in an African setting. Towards this end, the MRC team was granted privileged access to death reports as they streamed into Pretoria. The first results became available in 2001, and they ran thus: 339,000 adult deaths in 1998, 375,000 in 1999 and 410,000 in 2000.

This was grimly consistent with predictions of rising mortality, but the scale was problematic. Epimodel estimated 250,000 AIDS deaths in 1999, but there were only 375,000 adult deaths in total that year—far too few to accommodate the UN's [United Nation's] claims on behalf of the HIV virus. In short, Epimodel had failed its reality check. It was quietly shelved in favour of a more sophisticated local model, ASSA 600, which yielded a 'more realistic' death toll from AIDS of 143,000 for the calendar year 1999.

At this level, AIDS deaths were about 40 per cent of the total—still a bit high, considering there were only 232,000 deaths left to distribute among all other causes. The MRC team solved the problem by stating that deaths from ordinary disease had declined at the cumulatively massive rate of nearly 3 per cent per annum since 1985. This seemed very odd. How could deaths decrease in the face of new cholera and malaria epidemics, mounting poverty, the widespread emergence of drug-resistant killer microbes, and a state health system reported to be in 'terminal decline'?

But anyway, these researchers were experts, and their tinkering achieved the desired end: modelled AIDS deaths and real deaths were reconciled, the books balanced, truth revealed. The fruit of the MRC's ground-breaking labour was published in June 2001, and my hash appeared to have been settled. To be sure, I carped about curious adjustments and overall magnitude, but fell silent in the face of graphs showing huge changes in the *pattern* of death, with more and more people dying at sexually active ages. 'How can you argue with this?' cried my wife, eyes flashing angrily. I couldn't. I put my AIDS papers in the garage and ate my hat.

An Infallible Model?

But I couldn't help sneaking the odd look at science websites to see how the drama was developing. Towards the end of 2001, the vaunted ASSA 600 model was replaced by ASSA 2000, which produced estimates even lower than its predecessor: for the calendar year 1999, only 92,000 AIDS deaths in total. This was just more than a third of the original UN figure, but no matter; the boffins claimed ASSA 2000 was so accurate that further reference to actual death reports 'will be of limited usefulness'. A bit eerie, I thought, being told that virtual reality was about to render the real thing superfluous, but if these experts said the new model was infallible, it surely was infallible.

Only it wasn't. [In December 2002] ASSA 2000 was retired, too. A note on the MRC website explained that modelling was an inexact science, and that 'the number of people dying of AIDS has only now started to increase'. Furthermore, said the MRC, there was a new model in the works, one that would 'probably' produce estimates 'about 10 per cent lower' than those presently on the table. The exercise was not strictly valid, but I persuaded my scientist pal Rodney Richards to run the revised data on his own simulator and see what he came up with for 1999. The answer, very crudely, was an AIDS death toll somewhere around 65,000—a far cry indeed from the 250,000 initially put forth by UNAIDS.

The wife has just read this, and she is not impressed. 'It's obscene,' she says. 'You're treating this as if it's just a computer game. People are dying out there.'

Well, yes. I concede that. People are dying, but this doesn't spare us from the fact that AIDS in Africa is indeed something of a computer game. When you read that 29.4 million Africans are 'living with HIV/AIDS', it doesn't mean that millions of living people have been tested. It means that modellers assume that 29.4 million Africans are linked via enormously complicated mathematical and sexual networks to one of those women who tested HIV positive in those annual pregnancy-clinic surveys. Modellers are the first to admit that this exercise is subject to uncertainties and large margins of error. Larger than expected, in some cases. . . .

'The Worst May Be Over'

[Health policy analyst Paul] Bennell was able . . . to gather information about Africa's schoolteachers, usually described as a high-risk HIV group on account of their steady income, which enables them to drink and party more than others. [In 2002] World Bank claimed that AIDS was killing Africa's teachers 'faster than they can be replaced'. The BBC reported that 'one in seven' Malawian teachers would die in 2002 alone.

Bennell looked at the available evidence and found actual teacher mortality to be 'much lower than expected'. In Malawi, for instance, the all-causes death rate among schoolteachers was under 3 per cent, not over 14 per cent. In Botswana, it was about three times lower than computer-generated estimates. In Zimbabwe, it was four times lower. Bennell believes that AIDS continues to present a serious threat to educators, but concludes that 'overall impact will not be as catastrophic as suggested'. What's more, teacher deaths appear to be declining in six of the eight countries he has studied closely. 'This is quite unexpected,' he remarks, 'and suggests that, in terms of teacher deaths, the worst may be over.' In the past year or so, similar mutterings have been heard throughout southern Africa—the epidemic is levelling off or even declining in the worst-affected countries. UNAIDS has been at great pains to rebut such ideas, describing them as 'dangerous myths', even though the data on UNAIDS' own website shows they are nothing of the sort. 'The epidemic is not growing in most countries,' insists Bennell. 'HIV prevalence is not increasing as is usually stated or implied.'

The Manipulation of Fear

Bennell raises an interesting point here. Why would UNAIDS and its massive alliance of pharmaceutical companies, NGOs [non-governmental organizations], scientists and charities insist that the epidemic is worsening if it isn't? A possible explanation comes from New York physician Joe Sonnabend, one of the pioneers of AIDS research. Sonnabend was working in a New York clap clinic when the syndrome first appeared, and went on to found the American Foundation for AIDS Research, only to quit in protest when colleagues started exaggerating the threat of a generalised pandemic with a view to increasing AIDS' visibility and adding urgency to their grant applications. The AIDS establishment, says Sonnabend, is extremely skilled at 'the manipulation of fear for advancement in terms of money and power.'

With such thoughts in the back of my mind, South Africa's AIDS Day 'celebrations' cast me into a deeply leprous mood. Please don't get me wrong here. I believe that AIDS is a real problem in Africa. Governments and sober medical professionals should be heeded when they express deep concerns about it. But there are breeds of AIDS activist and AIDS journalist who sound hysterical to me. On AIDS Day, they came forth like loonies drawn by a full moon, chanting that AIDS was getting worse and worse, 'spinning out of control', crippling economies, causing famines, killing millions, contributing to the oppression of women, and 'undermining democracy' by sapping the will of the poor to resist dictators.

To hear them talk, AIDS is the only problem in Africa, and the only solution is to continue the agitprop until free access to AIDS drugs is defined as a 'basic human right' for everyone. They are saying in effect, that because Mr Mhlangu of rural Zambia has a disease they find more compelling than any other, someone must spend upwards of $400 a year to provide Mr Mhlangu with life-extending AIDS medication—a noble idea, on its face, but completely demented when you consider that Mr Mhlangu's neighbours are likely to be dying in much larger numbers of diseases that could be cured for a few cents if medicines were only available. About 350 million Africans—nearly half the population—get malaria every year, but malaria medication is not a basic human right. Two million get TB, but last time I checked, spending on AIDS research exceeded spending on TB by a crushing factor of 90 to one. As for pneumonia, cancer, dysentery or diabetes, let them take aspirin, or grub in the bush for medicinal herbs.

I think it is time to start questioning some of the claims made by the AIDS lobby. Their certainties are so fanatical, the powers they claim so far-reaching. Their authority is ultimately derived from computer-generated estimates, which they wield like weapons, overwhelming any resistance with dumbfounding atom bombs of hypothetical human misery. Give them their head, and they will commandeer all resources to fight just one disease. Who knows, they may defeat AIDS, but what if we wake up five years hence to discover that the problem has been blown-up out of all proportion by unsound estimates, causing upwards of $20 billion to be wasted?

Periodical Bibliography

The following articles have been selected to supplement the diverse views presented in this chapter.

Barry R. Bloom	"Lessons from SARS," *Science*, May 2, 2003.
Rachel Cohen	"An Epidemic of Neglect: Neglected Diseases and the Health Burden in Poor Countries," *Multinational Monitor*, June 2002.
Mary H. Cooper	"Fighting SARS," *CQ Researcher*, June 20, 2003.
Theodore Dalrymple	"Apocalypse Probably Postponed . . . ," *New Statesman*, April 28, 2003.
Economist	"Good News, Apparently: AIDS Statistics in Africa," January 17, 2004.
Simon Elegant	"What Other Bugs Are Out There?" *Time International*, April 7, 2003.
Richard G.A. Feachem	"The Real Enemy," *Washington Post National Weekly Edition*, January 20–26, 2003.
Gregory K. Folkers and Anthony S. Fauci	"AIDS Agenda Still Daunting," *Issues in Science and Technology*, Summer 2003.
Stephen S. Hall	"On the Trail of the West Nile Virus," *Smithsonian*, July 2003.
Melissa Healy	"Are Quarantines Back?" *Los Angeles Times*, April 14, 2003.
Wendy Johnson	"Microbes at the Gates," *Nation*, April 22, 2002.
Judith Walzer Leavitt and Lewis A. Leavitt	"After SARS: Fear and Its Uses," *Dissent*, Fall 2003.
Donald G. McNeil Jr. and Lawrence K. Altman	"How One Person Can Fuel an Epidemic," *New York Times*, April 15, 2003.
Siddhartha Mukherjee	"Oversight," *New Republic*, May 12, 2003.
Jeffrey Sachs	"Weapons of Mass Salvation," *Economist*, October 26, 2002.
Marilyn Werber Serafini	"States Wrestle with Quarantine Laws," *National Journal*, May 17, 2003.

What Can Be Done to Curtail the AIDS Epidemic?

Chapter Preface

Acquired immunodeficiency syndrome (AIDS) is one of the most devastating epidemics in modern history. Between 1981 and 2000, more than 20 million people worldwide had died of complications resulting from AIDS, and by the year 2004 at least 42 million people were living with the human immunodeficiency virus (HIV). In many parts of the world, AIDS remains the leading cause of death of people between the ages of eighteen and forty-four. Sub-Saharan Africa has been hit particularly hard by the virus, with an estimated 30 million people who are currently HIV positive. In Botswana 39 percent of the adult population is thought to be infected with the virus. A baby born today in Botswana has a life expectancy of thirty-two years, compared with an average of sixty-five years a decade ago.

In Africa the AIDS virus is generally presumed to be spread through sexual contact and from mother to child during pregnancy. Consequently, prevention efforts often focus on "risk-reduction" behavioral strategies such as promoting sexual abstinence before marriage, monogamy within marriage, or the use of condoms to curb the spread of the virus through sexual activity. Those who stress risk reduction, however, often differ on which particular strategy is most effective. Proponents of abstinence and fidelity maintain that traditional sexual morality is far more effective than condom use in stopping the spread of AIDS. Uganda is often cited as an example of the success of the abstinence-based policy. A decade ago, the HIV infection rate in Uganda was nearly 20 percent of the population; today it has decreased to less than 8 percent. Douglas A. Sylva, director of research at the Catholic Family and Human Rights Institute, asserts that "Uganda remains a lone success story" because "millions of Ugandans have embraced traditional sexual morality, including sexual abstinence outside of marriage and fidelity within marriage, in order to avoid infection." Conversely, Sylva points out, South Africa remains the world leader in AIDS infection despite an increase in condom use in that nation.

Critics of abstinence-focused strategies grant that Uganda's success in curtailing AIDS offers hope to other African nations. However, they contend that Uganda's victory is due to multiple factors. Along with a reduction in multiple sexual partnerships and a delaying of the age of first sexual activity, condom use has doubled among Ugandan women between the ages of fifteen and twenty-four. In addition, as United Nations officials point out, the gains in Uganda have been fostered "by a government mandate that every official discuss the epidemic in virtually every speech." International AIDS activists maintain that Uganda's success proves that a comprehensive approach—education about HIV and the various ways to avoid infection—is the best strategy. Many groups are critical, moreover, of the view that AIDS in Africa stems from a moral problem that can be solved by changing people's sexual behavior. According to a series of papers published by British Royal Society of Medicine, sexual transmission accounts for only one-third of Africa's AIDS cases. The rest, the authors assert, "can be attributed to unsanitary medical practices in health-care clinics, specifically the use of unclean needles," an activity that is common in poor nations.

How to best curtail the AIDS epidemic in Africa is one of several compelling controversies surrounding AIDS and public and international health policy. The authors in the following chapter discuss various methods for slowing or stopping the spread of HIV/AIDS.

"We are determined to turn the tide against AIDS."

Emergency Relief Is Needed to End the AIDS Epidemic

George W. Bush

In the following viewpoint George W. Bush summarizes his administration's emergency plan for combating AIDS in several third-world countries. The United States will donate 15 billion dollars between 2004 and 2009, focusing on providing antiretroviral drugs, expanding hospitals, and increasing access to HIV tests and AIDS prevention education. This plan will prevent 7 million new infections and extend the lives of at least 2 million people living with HIV, Bush explains. Bush is the forty-third president of the United States. This viewpoint is excerpted from a speech he delivered on January 31, 2003, in Washington, D.C.

As you read, consider the following questions:

1. On the continent of Africa, how many people under the age of fifteen have the AIDS virus, according to Bush?
2. According to the author, what is the Lazarus effect?
3. How are medications often delivered to far-flung villages and towns in Africa, according to Bush?

George W. Bush, "Remarks on the Emergency Plan for AIDS Relief," *Weekly Compilation of Presidential Documents*, vol. 39, February 3, 2003, p. 137.

This is a historic year for America. It's a year of great consequence. It's a year in which we have an opportunity to work with others to shape the future of our globe. We have a chance to achieve peace. We have a chance to achieve a more compassionate world for every citizen. America believes deeply that everybody has worth, everybody matters, everybody was created by the Almighty, and we're going to act on that belief, and we'll act on that passion.

You know, the world looks at us and says, "They're strong." And we are. We're strong militarily, but we've got a greater strength than that. We've got a strength in the universality of human rights and the human condition. It's in our country's history. It's ingrained in our soul. And today we're going to describe how we're going to act, not just talk, but act, on the basis of our firm beliefs. . . .

Responsibility and Freedom

We're a strong nation. But we're also a blessed nation. And it's important for our citizens to recognize that richness is one thing. Recognizing that we're blessed gives a different perspective, I think. I think it enhances the fact that we have a responsibility. If you're blessed, there is a responsibility to recognize your blessings in a compassionate way. Blessings are a two-way street. We've got to understand in this country that if you value life and say every life is equal, that includes a suffering child on the continent of Africa. If you're worried about freedom, that's just not freedom for your neighbor in America; that's freedom for people around the globe. It's a universal principle. . . .

Freedom is not America's gift to the world; freedom is God's gift to humanity. Freedom means freedom from a lot of things. And today, on the continent of Africa, freedom means freedom from the fear of a deadly pandemic. That's what we think in America, and we're going to act on that belief. Our founding belief in human dignity should be how we conduct ourselves around the world and will be how we conduct ourselves around the world.

I want you all to remember, and our fellow citizens to remember, that this is nothing new for our country. Human dignity has been a part of our history for a long time. We fed the hungry after World War I. This country carried out the Marshall plan and the Berlin airlift.[1]

Today we provide 60 percent—over 60 percent of all the international food aid. We're acting on our compassion. It's nothing new for our country. But there's a pandemic which we must address now, before it is too late. And that's why I took this message to our fellow citizens, that now is the time for this country to step up our efforts to save lives. After all, on the continent of Africa, 30 million people have the AIDS virus—30 million people. Three million children under the age of 15 have the AIDS virus. More than 4 million people require immediate drug treatment. Yet, just about one percent of people receive drug treatment. I mean, there is a significant world problem that the United States of America can do something about. We can be involved.

The Reality of the Pandemic

It's important for our fellow citizens . . . to understand that there are mass burials and unmarked graves on the continent of Africa. So many people are dying that the graves are unmarked. The pandemic is creating such havoc that there are mass burials, that there are wards of children that are dying because of AIDS, not a ward, not some wards, but wards after wards full of dying children because of AIDS, that there are millions of orphans, lonely children, because their mom or dad has died—children left, in some cases, to fend for themselves.

Because the AIDS diagnosis is considered a death sentence, many folks don't seek treatment, and that's a reality. It's as if the AIDS pandemic just continues to feed upon itself over and over and over again, because of hopelessness. This country needs to provide some hope, because this disease can be prevented and it can be treated. That's important for our fellow citizens to know. Antiretroviral drugs are now dramatically more affordable in many nations, and these drugs are used to extend the lives of those with HIV. In other

1. The Marshall plan was the U.S. strategy for reconstructing Europe after World War II. The 1948 Berlin airlift occurred after Russia closed rail lines and roads into West Berlin in an attempt to thwart economic prosperity in Allied zones. For eleven months, the Allies flew in supplies of food and fuel.

words, these drugs are really affordable.

And when the treatment has come to Africa, it is also important for our citizens to understand the effect of that treatment. It's called the Lazarus effect. When one patient is rescued by medicine, as if back from the dead, many others with AIDS seek testing and treatment, because it is the first sign of hope they have ever seen.

A Work of Mercy

We have the opportunity to bring that hope to millions. It's an opportunity for this Nation to affect millions and millions of lives. And so that's why I've laid out the Emergency Plan for AIDS Relief. I called it in my [2003] State of the Union a work of mercy, and that's what I believe it is.

With approval of Congress, we will devote $15 billion to fight AIDS abroad over the next 5 years, beginning with 2 billion in the year 2004. . . .

A Great Step Forward

President [George W.] Bush's recent commitment of significant new money and support to combat the AIDS epidemic in Africa and the Caribbean should be applauded as a great step forward for the United States. It is an opportunity for Americans to respond to a global health crisis with both compassion and impact, and not just with money but with effort . . .

With the new support, the United States can demonstrate to the international community that the problems that plague Africa can be solved, and that Africa is not too far away or too unimportant for other nations to become involved in the solutions.

Richard Marlink, *Hastings Center Report*, March/April 2003.

We're still committed to the Global AIDS Fund to fight disease. This program in no way diminishes our commitment to the fund. We will continue bilateral AIDS programs in more than 50 countries. We've already got bilateral relations with 50 countries with whom we're working on AIDS, and we'll continue that. . . .

But this plan that I've laid out in front of the Congress and will work with Members of the Senate and the House on will dramatically focus our efforts. You notice I didn't say, "focus our efforts," I said, "dramatically focus our efforts." And that's important for the American people to understand, because we want to bring a comprehensive system. It's more than money that we bring; we bring expertise and compassion and love and the desire to develop a comprehensive system, work with people in Africa to do so, for diagnosis and treatment and prevention.

We are determined to turn the tide against AIDS. And we're going to start in 14 African and Caribbean countries, where the disease is most heavily concentrated. We whip it in those . . . 14—we will show what is possible in other countries. . . .

We want to have intense focus where the need is most severe and show the world what is possible—not just show our fellow citizens or show the folks on the continent of Africa, but the world needs to see what we can do together. . . .

Where the Funding Will Go

The funding will initially go toward expanding existing hospitals and, of course, drawing on the knowledge and the expertise of local physicians. That makes sense. You've got a doc in place, we want to encourage that doc to be able to continue his or her healing. We'll build satellite facilities that can serve more people. Of course, we'll provide antiretroviral drugs and as well work with folks on the ground for education and care.

It's important for our citizens to know that the infrastructure is—it's hard for many Americans to imagine the lack of infrastructure that we're working with on the continent of Africa. So we use motorcycles, tracks, bicycles. We use nurses and local healers to go to the farthest villages and farms to test for the disease and to deliver medications that will save lives. It doesn't matter how the medications get there; what matters is they do get there.

Facilities across Africa and the Caribbean will have now the medicine. And our fellow citizens must understand that the reason they do is because of your generosity, the taxpayers of the country. I hope when our citizens absorb that knowledge—the massive attempt to save lives—that they feel proud of their country and proud of the compassion of

America. We're going to work with other governments, of course, private groups—there's all kinds of faith-based programs involved on the continent of Africa, and we welcome that, of course. And we encourage that. And we thank you for that. . . .

A Good Start

Here's what the experts believe that will be accomplished through the Emergency Plan for AIDS Relief: that in this decade, we will prevent 7 million new infections; that we'll treat at least 2 million people with life-extending drugs. We'll provide humane care, of course, for those who suffer and, as importantly, for the orphans.

To me, that's just the beginning. But it's a pretty good start. Most important thing is we're providing hope, which is immeasurable. How can you possibly measure the benefits of hope? There's no—we can't quantify that. But it certainly can be qualified by saying a hopeful society is a heck of a lot better society than what they found on the continent today.

This project is urgent, and as we move forward on this program we will continue to call upon other nations to join. The United States doesn't mind leading, and we believe others have a responsibility as well, that we're not the only blessed nation. There are many blessed nations. And we hope they join us. . . .

As we move forward into the 21st century, there's no doubt we can help the people on the African Continent, while we help our own folks at home with the deadly disease. There's no doubt we can arrest the pandemic. There's no doubt we can bring hope in all parts of the world, not only in Africa but in neighborhoods in our own country where people wonder what the American Dream means. There's no doubt in my mind we can make the world more peaceful.

"*The United States must work . . . to fund and organize the more comprehensive and critical effort of building sustainable health infrastructure.*"

A Long-Term Strategy Is Needed to End the AIDS Epidemic

Greg Behrman

Greg Behrman is the author of *The Invisible People: How the U.S. Has Slept Through the Global AIDS Pandemic, the Greatest Humanitarian Catastrophe of Our Time.* In the viewpoint that follows, Behrman argues that the United States must significantly increase its efforts to combat the AIDS epidemic. While the emergency plan initiated by the Bush administration in 2004 addresses some challenges, much more money and planning is needed to fund, build, equip, and staff health centers and clinics in poor countries. To turn the tide against AIDS, the United States must work with its international partners to create a viable health infrastructure in developing nations, Behrman concludes.

As you read, consider the following questions:

1. How many people are likely to be infected with the HIV virus by 2010, in Behrman's opinion?
2. According to the World Health Organization, what should the United States annually contribute by the year 2015 to fight AIDS?
3. Beyond assisting with the AIDS crisis, how would an improved health infrastructure benefit developing countries, according to Behrman?

[In February 2004] the Office of the U.S. Global AIDS Coordinator gave Congress its five-year strategic statement for enacting the Bush administration's $15-billion Emergency Plan for AIDS Relief. The plan seeks to "turn the tide of the global pandemic," and it is the boldest commitment ever to combat global AIDS. In its proposed form, however, it stands little chance of turning that tide.

The world knows no greater threat to human life than AIDS. Over the last 20 years, 25 million people around the globe have died of the disease. More than 40 million people are currently infected. Reasonable estimates predict that by this decade's end there will be 100 million or more global HIV infections, and 25 million AIDS orphans.

A Profound Threat

The disease is more than a humanitarian catastrophe, it is a moral crisis and a profound threat to U.S. and global security. It is beginning to eviscerate national economies. And the pandemic is generating social and political pressures that will soon threaten the integrity and viability of sub-Saharan African states. If they collapse, terrorists and transnational criminal elements will find refuge and sustenance in the debris.

The Bush administration's plan begins to address many of these challenges. It has specific near-term goals preventing 7 million new infections, treating 2 million infected people and caring for 10 million people over the next five years in some of the countries most acutely affected.

The plan's "emergency" posture highlights the importance of moving urgently and opportunistically to meet its goals. It uses local authorities, healthcare workers and community members to ensure that U.S. efforts cohere with local needs. All of these elements mean it should be able to produce much-needed near-term results.

The Missing Ingredient

The cardinal—and immeasurably fatal—flaw of the administration's program, however, is that it is only an emergency plan, not a long-term strategy to defeat global HIV/AIDS. The key missing ingredient is the building of health infrastructure.

Currently, a staggering global deficit in health centers, clinics, equipment and services, in healthcare workers and administrators, is crippling international efforts to combat the pandemic. Without robust health infrastructure, once the five-year plan runs its course and its targeted 2 million patients are under treatment, the affected countries will be no better off in their ability to test, treat and care for the additional tens of millions of people who will still be in desperate need of help.

Disturbing Data

The latest UNAIDS report has found that some prevention and treatment programs are under way in most countries coping with the [AIDS] epidemic, although they reach far too few people.

Some of the report's findings are as follows:

• Less than 1% of pregnant women in most sub-Saharan African nations receive information and treatment about avoiding transmission of HIV to their infants.

• Fewer than 5% of injecting drug users receive HIV prevention services.

• In 2002, only about 300,000 out of an estimated 5 million to 6 million HIV-infected people in low- and middle-income countries received antiretroviral medications when they needed them.

AIDS Alert, November 2003.

The president's initiative needs a simultaneous second track. The United States must work in concert with other countries, international institutions and nongovernmental organizations to fund and organize the more comprehensive and critical effort of building sustainable health infrastructure.

Funding Essential Interventions

The World Health Organization [WHO] Commission on Macroeconomics and Health found that essential health "interventions" could be met in the developing world with $34 per capita a year (the developed world spends more than $2,000 a year per capita on health). To meet that goal, WHO called for increased expenditures from the developing countries, but it also called for international donors to provide $27 billion a year by 2007 and, to meet increasing needs, $38 billion a year by 2015. The U.S. share would be roughly $9 billion a year by 2007 and $13 billion a year by 2015. For less than 10 cents of every $100 of gross national product, WHO estimated, $186 billion in economic output a year by 2015 would be generated through life extension and enhanced productivity. Most important, WHO found that by 2010 these efforts would be saving 8 million lives a year.

The developing world must be equipped to test, treat and counsel a huge number of patients in the decades ahead. Such capabilities would drive prevention as well.

In addition, a vast upgrade in health infrastructure could allow developing countries to tackle tuberculosis, malaria and their many other pressing health challenges. Healthier societies would strengthen these states' economies and institutions—the essential elements in a sustained battle against AIDS.

An Affordable Commitment

The United States and its international partners must move now. Much hangs in the balance. The commitment is affordable, the threat is dire and the opportunity is incomparable. In addressing the enormous need for health infrastructure, the United States and its international partners could chart a strategy that would save countless lives, provide a prodigious boost to global economic output and help safeguard the United States and people around the world from one of the gravest threats known to mankind.

"Abstinence and fidelity work to save lives."

Promoting Abstinence and Fidelity Would Curtail AIDS in Africa

Christianity Today

Proclaiming the biblical message to abstain or be faithful in marital relationships can greatly reduce the spread of AIDS in Africa, the editors of *Christianity Today* argue in the following viewpoint. So-called safe sex messages that encourage the use of condoms have been largely ineffective in preventing infections, the authors maintain. But field research proves that delaying the age of first sexual activity and reducing everyone's number of sexual partners decreases the spread of AIDS. The best way to promote such ideas is through the traditional Christian sexual ethic, which endorses abstinence and marital fidelity, the authors explain. *Christianity Today* is a weekly journal of evangelical Christian opinion.

As you read, consider the following questions:

1. How many people have AIDS in southern Africa, according to the authors?
2. According to Ray Martin, what two actions can demonstrate that Westerners care about AIDS in Africa?
3. What happened to Princess Kasune Zulu when she found out she was HIV-positive, according to the authors?

The blight of HIV/AIDS is worse than ever. Fresh estimates reveal that 1.2 percent of the world's population (age 15–49) is infected with HIV/AIDS. That's 74 million people. But in southern Africa, the rate is 18 times higher at 21.6 percent, giving the region the dreadful distinction of being the world's most infected area with nearly 11 million people with HIV/AIDS.

This deadly virus takes the strong and leaves the weak. In African families, when both parents have died, millions of orphaned brothers and sisters rely on grandparents or other blood relatives, or they fend for themselves. But tragically, the motivations of some relatives are not pure. "We get a lot of cases of property grabbing where family members . . . leave the children with nothing," a Botswana social worker said recently in comments to the Johannesburg news media.

HIV/AIDS is growing rapidly in many nations that have had a low rate of infection. The CIA's National Intelligence Council reported that the "next wave" will occur in Nigeria, Ethiopia, India, Russia, and China, which collectively represent 40 percent of the global population. More startling was the council's frank admission: "Avoidance of high-risk behavior is the only proven way to prevent the disease." This conclusion goes counter to 20 years of failed attempts to fight HIV/AIDS, mostly with billions upon billions of low-cost condoms (rarely used consistently) and costly drug cocktails (hard to administer and distribute fairly).

Abstinence and Fidelity

Christians in North America should note the sea change that is taking place in the public health community about HIV/AIDS prevention, opening a historic opportunity for outreach. New field research in Uganda, Senegal, and Jamaica shows that the spread of HIV/AIDS can be sharply reduced by:
- Delaying the age of "sexual debut" (when an individual first becomes sexually active).
- Reducing the number of sexual partners people have. In Christian terms, that means saving sex until you are married, and then remaining faithful to your spouse. "Zero grazing" is how church leaders in Uganda colorfully describe these standards at village-level workshops.

Edward C. Green, associated with the Harvard School of Public Health, has written a paper ("What Happened in Uganda?") based on his field research. Green notes that public health agencies have mostly paid lip service to the so-called A-B-C (Abstain, Be Faithful, or use a Condom) strategy. Globally, public-health officials have put far too much emphasis on condoms and drugs. Green says those two methods do not motivate "primary behavior change," in the same way as abstinence before marriage and marital fidelity.

Eliminating the Risk of Disease

Our critics often claim that chastity and sexual abstinence programs cannot work alone or at all. They claim that people cannot change their behavior, while at the same time they call for exactly that—for people to use condoms consistently and correctly every time they engage in sexual activity. If society is going to seek to modify conduct, then would it not be better and more effective to encourage behaviors such as chastity and abstinence that eliminate the risk of disease while promoting human dignity and a healthy life in all dimensions rather than behaviors that do not eradicate the risk of disease and lull people into a false sense of security?

Theodore McCarrick, *Origins*, June 19, 2003.

Commenting on HIV/AIDS, Samaritan's Purse president Franklin Graham [stated], "The number one obstacle is the world's concept: Just give me a billion condoms and we can solve this issue."

But Graham went on to suggest another problem, this one with the church: "What the world wants to do is to continue in their sinful lifestyle. The church is sitting back, saying, 'I told you so. If you all would keep your pants zipped up, then there wouldn't be any of these problems.'"

Prevention and Practical Care

Fortunately, more Christians and their churches have stepped forward to care for the sick, the dying, and their children. Now that HIV/AIDS is out of control across the world, churches—especially in North America—have much more to do beyond caring for those already infected.

"Faith-based organizations are best positioned of any

group to promote fidelity and abstinence," says Green. "There are insufficient programs directed at partner reduction and delay of sexual debut among youth. [Faith-based organizations] remain an untapped potential."

In a world desperate for a solution to HIV/AIDS, Christians and their congregations needn't be shy in publicly proclaiming the biblical message that abstinence and fidelity work to save lives. There are legitimate needs for orphan care and for people who are HIV-positive. Christians worldwide are unrivaled in their potential to be model communities, coherently teaching sound sexual ethics to young and old.

Ray Martin, a retired official with the federal agency USAID, works with Christian professionals in public health. Martin recalled that during a recent meeting with Africans, "The first thing they were asking for wasn't money for drugs or money to expand programs; it was a plea to us, in this rich country where we're not faced with all this mortality, to care."

Martin suggests two ways to demonstrate care: Travel and partnership. "When you really see firsthand what people are dealing with, it makes a difference," he says. "Treasury Secretary [Paul] O'Neill visited Africa with [rock star] Bono and what he saw in Africa got through."

More churches should refocus mission visits on areas hit hard by HIV/AIDS. Second, Martin believes congregations that "twin" with churches on the frontline are a powerfully positive force. Christ Presbyterian Church in Edina, Minnesota, and the Balm in Gilead movement are setting the pace for compassionate, practical care in partnership.

In addition, the global fight against HIV/AIDS needs to find a place in the budget priorities of American congregations. "How much money do you have in your budget for HIV/AIDS?" Franklin Graham asks. "Make it a line item so that the elders and the deacons and the pastor, everybody, sees it."

Changing Attitudes

As faithful Christians break the stigma surrounding HIV/AIDS, attitudes will change. In Zambia, Princess Kasune Zulu found out she was HIV-positive at age 22. She was kicked out of her church and Moffat, her HIV-positive husband, lost his job. But she began caring for families hit by AIDS, working through the Hope Initiative, and hosting the Positive Living radio program. Zulu's activism demonstrates how HIV-positive Christians are one of the church's most potent resources in this fight.

The "safe sex" message has largely been a miserable failure in preventing increased infection worldwide. The church's message urgently needs stronger backing. Getting the word out about abstinence and fidelity will take more than the right message. It will take credible persuasion and global proclamation.

"We need to build a new culture that will promote equality, mutual respect, mutual decision-making and mutual responsibility in sexual relations."

Promoting Gender Equality Would Curtail AIDS in Africa

Ndivhuwo Masindi

Strategies promoting abstinence, faithfulness, or the use of condoms to fight AIDS in Africa are ineffective, contends Ndivhuwo Masindi in the following viewpoint. Encouraging abstinence does not work in countries where many girls and women are coerced or pressured into unsafe sexual activity, she points out. Moreover, preaching fidelity is largely futile in cultures where men often feel entitled to have several sexual partners. On the other hand, condom use contradicts African social traditions, which emphasize the importance of children and large families, explains Masindi. A more effective strategy would be to offer education that challenges outmoded norms, encourages honest dialogue about sexuality, and promotes equality between men and women. Masindi is a senior trainer with the Women's Health Project at the University of Witwatersrand in Johannesburg, South Africa.

As you read, consider the following questions:
1. What is the "ABC" strategy of fighting AIDS, according to Masindi?
2. According to the author, what often happens when African women try to get men to use condoms?
3. What is the Sexual Rights Campaign, according to Masindi?

Ndivhuwo Masindi, "Challenging Sexual Norms with the Sexual Rights Campaign," *Sister Namibia*, vol. 14, May/June 2002, p. 10. Copyright © 2002 by *Sister Namibia*. Reproduced by permission.

The human race is faced with a new straggle or freedom: freedom from HIV and AIDS. Every one of us is beginning to have intimate experiences of the disease—through living with it ourselves, through a family member who is dying of AIDS, through the orphans in our neighborhoods. We are traumatised and distressed because of multiple bereavements in our own families, and the stigma is breaking down our community values such that many people are being left to die alone.

For many years we have done educational programmes promoting the strategies of ABC (Abstain–Be faithful–Condomise), and still the infection rate has soared. In the meantime our hopes for vaccines and microbicides have not yet materialised, and anti-retrovirals currently remain beyond our reach. Education therefore still remains our only tool in our struggle against the pandemic.

However, we are now challenged to unpack and analyse what the educational programmes promoting ABC haven't offered us so far. We have spoken continuously about abstinence, about 'being faithful' or using condoms without analysing what happens when people close their bedroom doors. This didn't raise the issue of who our custodians in our bedrooms are, who decides what should happen and whether to use a condom or not.

Cultural Barriers to the ABC Strategy

We therefore need to launch a campaign that speaks to the social and cultural barriers to the ABC strategy we have promoted for so long with little success. We need to develop a strategy that will enable us to examine our traditional values of sexual relations and challenge how we live our sexuality within our own communities.

Let's start by analysing the call for abstinence: how does this fit into our values of sex? We know from research that in the Southern African region, most of us as women experienced our first sexual relationship as forced or coerced, either directly or indirectly.

Very few of us decided that 'today is the day I feel I am ready to engage in sexual relations.' We are living in a society where there is a lot of peer pressure to engage in sexual relations among the youth, where raping girls is seen as cool, where boys believe that 'making a baby is proving your fertility and you can try to prove your fertility with many girls and there is nothing wrong about it'. Promoting abstinence without challenging these sexual norms and values is obviously not a useful strategy.

We talk about 'being faithful' in a society that has normalised multiple sexual partners for men, whether married or single. We condone this as long as he provides financially, and we ask our sisters and daughters "is he not still buying mealie meal? Is he not coming back home at night?" But we don't go further and say "you are standing a risk of contracting HIV and AIDS."

There is a growing trend of older married men having sexual relations with young women. This is taking place in the context of a society that is very poor but has access to the global images of youth having beautiful jeans, a cell phone and cash to boast around with friends. These older men might have had more than sixty sexual partners in their lives, but because they are providing financially they are dictating the terms in their relationship with a girl who is in a weak position to negotiate for safer sex.

This also puts our young men at risk, as the young women may also have relationships with boyfriends of their age.

Custodians of the Condom

Let us come to the issue of using condoms. How can we use condoms when we feel that we still need to give birth, either to avoid being cursed by our parents who value large families, or because our family name needs to be passed on, or because we need to maintain a population dying out from AIDS?

We need to seriously question all those messages. Getting pregnant means unprotected sex; sex without a condom, which not only allows the sperm cell to travel from one body to another but also the HIV virus. Women and men are still deciding to have a baby without considering an HIV test as part of the decision-making, and we will continue to see babies dying at 4 or 6 weeks until we have overcome the stigma of testing for HIV and AIDS.

While men are still considered the custodians of sexual

norms who sanction everything that happens in the bed-room, women's negotiations for using condoms are often met with hostility, threats of desertion, even physical violence. And the very same women who are threatened with desertion are living in a society that says 'you are not woman enough if you are not married, you are not woman enough if you do not have a child, you are not woman enough if you do not have a man above you to control you.' We are living in a society where a woman will never have a status unless there is a man signed in to give her that status.

The Problem with Risk-Reduction Strategies

The ABC [Abstain, Be Faithful, Condomize] policy . . . ignores the plight of married women who are faithful to their husbands, but are powerless to ask that he wear a condom even when he is known to have acquired HIV infection.

"When we look at the ABC strategy, it's not going to empower women to prevent HIV infection because many women do abstain, and they say their sole sexual experience was with their husband," says Bella Matambanadzo, executive director at the Zimbabwe Resource Center and Network in Harare.

"These women say, 'I was a virgin when I got married, and now I'm HIV-positive,'" she says. "They say, 'I was wise. I waited, got married, so are you telling me that I was unwise?'"

AIDS Alert, May 2004.

These are some of the many challenges that we as communities, as a society are faced with. We need to find ways to engage one another in dialogue, not only to analyse cultural values of masculinity and femininity, but to redefine sexuality such that sex is not only considered as a pleasurable thing for men, but as a positive and pleasurable experience for both men and women.

Building a New Culture

We need to build a new generation of men who no longer commercialise sex, not only by using the services of sex workers, but by making sex a man's right in marriage and a price for a woman to pay for all that he is providing for the family. We need to build a new group of men who will use condoms not only with casual sexual partners but with their wives or girlfriends. We need to build a new group of men who will stop harassing women at the work place. Gender inequality is rife in our institutions, with most of the senior positions still occupied by men, making women vulnerable to sexual exploitation such as giving sex for a promotion.

We need to build a new group of women who know and claim their sexual rights; women who believe in themselves that they have the right to choose with whom, when and how to have sex, according to what would make them enjoy it most. We need to build a new group of women who will break the silence around sexual violence; who are going to report rape and incest; women who feel confident to negotiate for safer sex and refuse to submit to hostility, threats, coercion and violence. We also need to build a society where each and every individual will be able to express and exercise his or her sexual orientation without being victims of diverse ideological complexities.

We need to build a new culture that will promote equality, mutual respect, mutual decision-making and mutual responsibility in sexual relations. We need to declare access to sexual health information as a right, and break barriers such as virginity testing that aim at controlling girls' bodies while denying them access to sexual health information. We need to declare access to sexual health services as a right and challenge authoritarian relationships between the health provider and the clients. Women and men who experience sexually transmitted diseases are often called names within our health system, and are blamed as irresponsible and ignorant.

We also need to revisit the policies that exist in our countries that disempower us; policies that have defined reproductive rights over sexual rights, therefore denying the rights of people who don't do sex for procreation. We need to scrap policies that stigmatise and criminalise sex work, preventing sex workers from accessing health services. We further need to challenge policies that deny women the right to decide when to have a child; the right to exercise control over their body; policies that deny women access to safe abortion services.

The Sexual Rights Campaign

We in South Africa launched the Sexual Rights Campaign in 1999. It is a joint effort by NGOs [non-governmental organizations] and government departments. Together we are creating space for dialogue and action around all the issues raised above and many more. We are mobilising policy makers, educators, health workers, police officers, traditional leaders, religious leaders, women's groups, men's groups, people from different sexual orientations to identify and challenge the cultural barriers hindering our struggle against HIV and AIDS.

We are hoping to launch a Sexual Rights Charter . . . where people from different ministries and constituencies will come together to define sexual rights and develop strategies for addressing barriers to mutual respect in sexual decision-making in all sectors of our society.

"It is essential that people with HIV learn their status early so they can receive drugs to delay the onset of AIDS."

Access to Rapid HIV Tests Should Be Expanded

Arleen Leibowitz, Stephanie Taylor, and Jonathan Fielding

Arleen Leibowitz is a professor of policy studies at the University of California in Los Angeles and a member of the UCLA Center for HIV Identification, where Stephanie Taylor is a fellow. Jonathan Fielding, the health officer for Los Angeles County, is a pediatrics professor at UCLA. In the following viewpoint Leibowitz, Taylor, and Fielding argue that OraQuick, a rapid HIV-testing method, should be made widely available through the use of mobile vans. The authors point out that rapid testing would enable many HIV-positive people to start receiving treatment earlier and begin curtailing sexual activity that could transfer the virus.

As you read, consider the following questions:
1. How quickly does the OraQuick test provide results, according to the authors?
2. According to the authors, how is the OraQuick test conducted?
3. What is one of three elements in the CDC's strategic plan to reduce HIV infections, according to the authors?

There was a major victory in the battle against HIV/ AIDS recently when the Food and Drug Administration [FDA] approved the first easy-to-use "rapid" test for HIV, called OraQuick. This test provides results in about 20 minutes instead of the two days to two weeks required with standard HIV tests.

Unfortunately, the FDA approved the test for use only in facilities with certified laboratories. This requirement excludes OraQuick testing in mobile vans and at other sites that serve low-income and uninsured populations.

Reliable and Safe

Can the rapid test be safely conducted in sites without a certified laboratory, such as mobile vans? The rapid test, available in more than 90 countries, is no more difficult to use than at-home glucose tests for diabetes.

To conduct the OraQuick HIV test, a person pricks his or her finger and places a drop of blood in a vial, mixing it with a solution. The test kit is then inserted into the vial. In 20 minutes or less, two reddish-purple lines in the test's window will indicate whether the blood is infected with the HIV virus.

The test is remarkably reliable, with very small percentages of false negative or false positive results. Nonetheless, any positive test is confirmed with the standard tests that are currently in use.

The Benefits of Rapid Testing

Los Angeles County provides free and convenient HIV testing in mobile vans for those who are at significant risk. But under the current system, clients served by these vans must return at a later date to receive their HIV test results.

Results of a 1999 county survey found that 25% of those who obtained their HIV test in a mobile medical van did not return for their results. In contrast, 9% of those who were tested in their doctor's office and 11% of those who were tested in family planning or community clinics failed to learn the results of their HIV test.

The percentage of clients receiving results would be greatly increased if it were possible to use the OraQuick test to provide results on the spot.

The benefits of rapid testing extend to other nontraditional sites for health-care delivery, such as county jails. The transient nature of the jail population makes it imperative to provide results as quickly as possible to the tested inmates.

It is essential that people with HIV learn their status early so they can receive drugs to delay the onset of AIDS. Further, it is important that testing be accompanied by counseling to assist clients in reducing risky behavior.

The Importance of Testing

Nine out of 10 people living with HIV/AIDS do not know they are infected. Yet studies show that young people have a strong interest in knowing their HIV status.

Voluntary and confidential HIV counseling and testing is an important tool for preventing HIV. This allows adolescents to evaluate their behavior and its consequences. For example, a negative test result offers a key opportunity for a counselor to reinforce the importance of safety and risk-reduction behaviors. Young people who test positive for HIV must receive referrals for medical care and must talk to individuals who can help them understand what their HIV-positive status means as well as the responsibilities they have to themselves and others.

SIECUS Report, October/November 2002.

Recognizing the importance of counseling and testing, the federal Centers for Disease Control and Prevention [CDC] has established testing to promote early diagnosis as one of the three elements in a strategic plan to reduce annual HIV infections by half within five years. The rapid test will probably be less costly, further enhancing the CDC's efforts to increase testing.

The FDA should approve the manufacturer's application to waive restrictions limiting use of the OraQuick rapid test to laboratories. That federal agency's approval [in November 2002] of three at-home glucose tests for diabetes provides a relevant and timely precedent for granting such a waiver.[1]

The many positive benefits of early identification of

---

1. The FDA issued a special waiver in January 2003.

people who are HIV-positive argue for dissemination of the rapid-test technology to mobile vans and other sites without a certified laboratory.

Informing those who are HIV-positive of their status not only allows them to begin early treatment with effective antiretroviral medications, it can result in reduction of behavior that carries risk of transmitting HIV.

"When the government uses [rapid HIV tests] in bathhouses, it will mean we have sued for peace with the behavior that spreads a lethal virus."

Access to Rapid HIV Tests Should Be Limited

Terence P. Jeffrey

Government funds should not be used to offer rapid HIV tests at sex clubs and bathhouses, argues Terence P. Jeffrey in the following viewpoint. While quick HIV test results could certainly be of benefit to many people, offering federally funded tests at bathhouses means that taxpayers will be forced to pay some of the health care costs of those who knowingly engage in dangerous and immoral behavior, Jeffrey contends. Americans must reexamine their government's approach to HIV prevention if they seriously intend to curb the AIDS epidemic, he concludes. Jeffrey is a nationally syndicated columnist and the editor of *Human Events*, a weekly conservative paper.

As you read, consider the following questions:
1. According to the Kaiser Family Foundation, how much did the federal government spend on HIV/AIDS in 2002?
2. According to Jeffrey, what is the annual number of U.S. AIDS deaths?
3. What kinds of people might benefit from access to a rapid HIV test, in Jeffrey's opinion?

In the war against HIV, the deadly virus that causes AIDS, we are fast approaching Appomattox. Only this time, it isn't the rebels waving the white flag, it's the federal government; and this time the surrender won't be sealed with a signature in a country house, it will be sealed with a federally funded 20-minute HIV test administered in a sex club or bathhouse.

"Since the early 1990s, an estimated 40,000 new HIV infections have occurred annually in the United States," the federal Centers for Disease Control and Prevention (CDC) reported [in April 2003] in its *Morbidity and Mortality Weekly Report* (MMWR).

The Failure of Federal Efforts

The high incidence of infection has persisted despite massive increases in federal spending to fight the virus. The Kaiser Family Foundation reports that federal spending on HIV/AIDS increased from $3.1 billion (in non-inflation-adjusted dollars) in 1990 to $14.7 billion in 2002. (President [George W.] Bush has requested $16 billion for domestic HIV/AIDS spending [in 2004] and $2 billion more to fight HIV/AIDS abroad.)

Between 1995 and 2002—while 40,000 Americans were infected annually—federal spending targeted specifically at preventing HIV infection jumped 45%, from $639 million to $925 million.

Increased spending did not decrease infections. Clearly, federal HIV-prevention efforts are failing and must be re-examined.

While U.S. policy has inspired better technologies in response to HIV, it has not inspired better behavior. Self-destructive activity has achieved a strategic balance with medical science. Despite new drugs, says the MMWR, "The annual number of incident AIDS cases and deaths have remained stable since 1998, at approximately 40,000 and 16,000 respectively."

This has become a war of attrition. Barring a fundamental change in tactics, the casualty count will mount.

But the government's latest response not only recapitulates the failed approach of the past, it reduces it to the absurd.

America has developed another miracle technology: a rapid HIV test called OraQuick. In 20 minutes it can determine if HIV antibodies are present in a pinprick of blood. In January [2003], the Food and Drug Administration issued a special waiver allowing the test to be used in what it discretely called "outreach settings." In June [2003], the CDC announced it would purchase 250,000 test kits for $2 million and distribute them to local health organizations. News reports indicated the tests could be used in bathhouses and sex clubs. Indeed, CDC guidelines seemed to say the owners of such places would become "key partners" in the program.

Bathhouses and Sex Clubs

Although they are small in number, bathhouses have an impressive reach. One survey found only about 80 bathhouses and sex clubs in the entire United States. But a recent study of gay men in major cities revealed that nearly one-third had visited such a place in the previous year. Furthermore, surveys of men who frequent baths confirm what their surroundings encourage: On average, bathhouse patrons have had sex with more than 30 different men in the previous six months. Baths can serve thousands of men per week, and major gay gatherings such as New Orleans' "Decadence" and Mardi Gras attract men from all over the country. Not surprisingly, this makes them critical hotspots for the spread of sexually transmitted diseases, including HIV.

Tom Farley, *Washington Monthly*, November 2002.

"Agreements with law enforcement, owners of social venues such as bathhouses or sex clubs, neighborhood associations, and other key partners should be established before testing activities begin," advised the CDC in a document titled "Advancing HIV Prevention: Interim Technical Guidance for Selected Intervention."

Sex-Club Socialism

I called the CDC to confirm that the federally funded rapid HIV tests could be used in, among other places, bathhouses and sex clubs. CDC spokesperson Karlie Stanton confirmed that they could.

This is not compassionate conservatism. It is sex-club socialism. It transfers to all taxpayers some of the cost incurred by unrepentant practitioners of reckless behavior. It will work no better than previous federal efforts to fight HIV.

Certainly, the rapid HIV test has valuable applications. It can be used, for example, to determine the status of previously untested mothers giving birth, helping save their babies. It can be used to determine when health care workers have been exposed. And it can relieve anxiety, and speed treatment, for those who go to clinics determined to be tested and to change their behavior.

But when the government uses it in bathhouses, it will mean we have sued for peace with the behavior that spreads a lethal virus.

Tellingly, CDC guidelines for counseling HIV test-takers recommend that counselors take "nonjudgmental" approach focusing on "HIV risk reduction," not risk elimination.

"For clients with several high-risk behaviors," say the guidelines, "the counselor should help clients focus on reducing the most critical risk they are willing to commit to changing. The step does not need to be a personal behavior change."

In the war against terrorism, America took a clear moral stand. You are either with or against us in resisting the senseless destruction of human life. Until we face with similar moral clarity the behaviors that spread HIV, the virus will continue to defeat us.

*"Social condemnation is, in fact, just about
the only realistic measure that can be taken
to combat [dangerous] behavior."*

Social Condemnation Is Needed to Curtail the AIDS Epidemic

Rod Dreher

A segment of the male homosexual population is intentionally engaging in unprotected sex, writes Rod Dreher in the following viewpoint. Such behavior has increased in recent years, with gay men increasingly participating in orgies and "conversion parties," in which HIV-negative men seek to contract AIDS through sex with HIV-positive men. These activities thwart efforts to stop the spread of AIDS and are a burden to taxpayers and the health care industry, Dreher argues. He concludes that gay male society deserves blame for refusing to denounce those who are willingly spreading the epidemic. Dreher is an editorial writer and columnist for the *Dallas Morning News*.

As you read, consider the following questions:
1. What is the annual health-care cost of treating a patient who is HIV-positive, according to Dreher?
2. What is "barebacking," according to the author?
3. What did some cities do to curb anonymous gay sex during the first wave of the AIDS epidemic, according to Dreher?

Rod Dreher, "Beds, Bathhouses, and Beyond: The Return of Public Sex," *National Review*, vol. 54, August 12, 2002, p. 15. Copyright © 2002 by National Review, Inc., 215 Lexington Ave., New York, NY 10016. Reproduced by permission.

When Harvard AIDS researcher Dr. Bruce Walker made his startling announcement to colleagues on July 10 [2002], the scientists filling the room at the 14th International Conference on AIDS audibly gasped. Dr. Walker revealed the case of an HIV-positive Boston man whose immune system had been doing an extraordinary job fighting the infection on its own. Then the man had unprotected sex with a male partner who was infected with a different strain of HIV.

"He never got a new [immune] response against the second virus, and he declined clinically," Dr. Walker said. "The public-health implication of this is that it is possible to become infected with a second strain of HIV, even a very closely related one."

This has, as one scientist put it, "shattering implications" for the development of an AIDS vaccine. In plain terms, it means the HIV virus is so mutable and durable that the standard method of vaccine-making will almost certainly not work.

Clearly, AIDS is going to be with us for a long time. And it's going to cost a lot of money. Another study presented at the AIDS conference found that the annual cost of treating a single patient in the advanced stages of AIDS is $34,000, and $14,000 for those who are HIV-positive but still healthy. According to the latest Centers for Disease Control numbers, as many as 900,000 Americans are living with either HIV or full-blown AIDS.

Gay Male Promiscuity

The situation is grim and getting grimmer. Just don't tell the gay-male community, or at least a significant portion of it. Many are partying like there's no tomorrow—and guaranteeing that for an untold number, there won't be.

"Gay Sluts Are Back," read the headline in the June 26 [2002], Gay Pride issue of the *San Francisco Bay Guardian*. The article, by self-described "gay slut" Simon Sheppard, celebrated the renascence of promiscuity among Bay Area homosexuals: "The threat of HIV was (and is) real and deadly. But the epidemic was also seized on as an instrument of control, by assimilationists within the queer community who wanted us all to behave like good girls and by those in the larger heterocentrist culture who were both envious of and repelled by men who numbered their sex partners in the dozens. Or hundreds. Or thousands."

The article characterized efforts by AIDS-prevention experts to dampen male promiscuity as hatred of sex and male desire. To ignore the problem, the argument goes, is to be both moral (since fulfilling sexual desire is the greatest good) and authentic. "There's been a quantum increase in unprotected anal sex, not only between those already HIV-infected but also among the not-yets," Sheppard wrote. "People who work in AIDS-prevention programs will confirm what we all already knew: queer men are having more sex, and less of it is condomized." He went on to praise the joy of "unapologetic homo-lust."

Orgies and Barebacking

Meanwhile, in New York, the AIDS capital of America, a city that has over four times the number of AIDS cases (122,000) as San Francisco (28,000), the Gay Pride issue of the *Village Voice* came with a headline touting "The Return of Public Sex." Mind you, this was not a lament. Writer Steve Weinstein opened his report from a penthouse party where a crowd of men in their twenties had paid $20 to participate in a private orgy. Then he went to a "dimly lit Midtown hotel suite" where 18 men were having an orgy; next, to a tugboat near Chelsea Piers, which men were using for anonymous sex. "After years of AIDS anxiety and government repression," he wrote, "gay public sex is bigger and better than ever."

The Internet is making this possible. Finding out where orgies are being held in your city on any given day is as easy as checking the Dow. Worse, some of these affairs are so-called "barebacking" events, which Michelangelo Signorile, a leading gay columnist, described five years ago as "quite common." Barebacking is the term used to describe unprotected anal sex. The risk of contracting HIV rises dramatically with condomless sex, of course; it's the danger that makes this kind of sex so exciting to its practitioners. Then there's the conviction that with protease-inhibiting drugs, AIDS is a manageable disease.

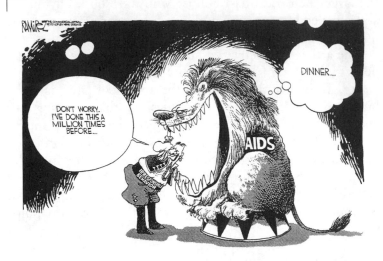

Ramirez. © 1993 by Copley News Service. Reproduced by permission.

Even more perverse are so-called "conversion parties," in which HIV-negative men willingly submit to sexual intercourse with AIDS-infected partners. In the argot of the gay sexual underworld, this is called "giving the gift," and those looking to become infected with HIV are called "bug chasers." A variation on this theme are "Russian Roulette parties," which consist of bareback orgies with HIV-positive and uninfected men, whose HIV status may not, by mutual consent, be known before the sex begins.

Because condomless sex is still considered an outlaw practice, researchers say it's impossible to tell with any accuracy how much of it is occurring. But a few studies, as well as anecdotal evidence, suggest that it is on the rise, and a sharp increase in the reported number of AIDS and other sexually transmitted disease cases bears this out. In May 2001, the Centers for Disease Control released a study indicating that a second massive wave of AIDS infections, comparable to the first wave of the 1980s, was about to sweep the homosexual population.

A Conspicuous Silence

A few prominent gay voices have broken the taboo on criticizing the sexual behavior of fellow homosexuals, and have been attacked by other gays as anti-sex and even homopho-bic. Gabriel Rotello, in his 1997 book *Sexual Ecology: AIDS and the Destiny of Gay Men*, bluntly stated that "people will have to accept the fact that the unlimited, unstructured pur-suit of absolute sexual freedom was biologically disastrous for gay men." He warned that it takes only a small number of gay men who engage in unprotected sex with multiple partners to keep the epidemic alive. Michelangelo Signorile, exasperated by the devil-may-care promiscuity of many fel-low homosexuals, wondered, "How will we continue to get hard-fought funding from the government, and compassion from our liberal friends, when they learn that a small but growing group of people within our own community are be-having recklessly and selfishly? How can many lesbians and a great many gay men themselves not throw their hands in the air, rightly disgusted and anguished?"

It turns out that Signorile was unduly worried. He posed those questions in 1997. Since then, there has been no hint that AIDS funding will be reduced or compassion lessened. We have now reached the point where gay promiscuity and bareback orgies can be praised in the pages of major left-wing newspapers as a return to the good old days. While the more mainstream media outlets would never publish articles prais-ing this suicidal phenomenon, they have been conspicuously silent about it, and they have not helped build the kind of public outrage among responsible gays and straights that might stand a chance of curtailing these practices. Imagine how the phenomenon would be reported if, in the middle of a deadly typhus epidemic, people were keeping the epidemic going by getting together to exchange infected lice for fun and pleasure. How would the newspapers report it? What would the public say? How would the government react?

The Only Realistic Measure

Social condemnation is, in fact, just about the only realistic measure that can be taken to combat this behavior. During the first wave of the AIDS epidemic, some city governments, including San Francisco's, closed the gay bathhouses, where public, anonymous sex was common, and which therefore served as incubators of the plague. This time, though, it is much more difficult to devise measures to crack down on public sex. For one thing, many barebacking parties occur in private residences. For another, a man craving anonymous sex need not risk arrest by prowling in public toilets or city parks for his fix; he has only to log on to the Internet, where willing partners and private locations for trysts are only a few mouse-clicks away.

One is tempted to think: So what? What goes on behind closed doors is nobody's business. This is fatally wrong. Aside from the fact that it's inhumane to remain indifferent while people blithely kill themselves, there is the not-insignificant matter of the enormous cost to the taxpayer and the health-care system. And, much more important, the mutation of HIV into newer and deadlier forms of the virus—a process aided by sex between HIV-positive men infected by different strains—has made an AIDS vaccine an even more remote possibility. The unavoidable truth is that male homosexual life has, in some quarters, become a death cult. Yet no one dares to hold gay-male society accountable for the nihilistic, erotomaniacal subculture that sustains the killing and dying. At the beginning of the third decade of the AIDS epidemic, the band, it seems, is still playing on: same song, second sad verse.

*"The radical potential of education to
promote safer . . . sex and to effect change
remains unfulfilled."*

Improved Education Is Needed to Curtail the AIDS Epidemic

Peter Aggleton

Education about HIV/AIDS must be updated and improved to help stop the spread of the epidemic, contends Peter Aggleton in the following viewpoint. For too long, AIDS education has focused on teaching people certain facts and skills without addressing emotional factors and cultural and socioeconomic differences. In addition, AIDS education programs have largely ignored the condemnation and rejection of those with HIV and AIDS, Aggleton points out. Educators need to understand the variety of contexts in which HIV/AIDS exists and find ways to empower communities to fight the epidemic. Aggleton is a professor of education at the University of London in England.

As you read, consider the following questions:

1. How might notions of honor affect one's sexual self-understanding, in Aggleton's opinion?
2. In the author's view, what five approaches to AIDS education need to be reexamined?
3. What is wrong with the "liberal enlightenment" model of AIDS education, according to Aggleton?

Peter Aggleton, "HIV/AIDS Prevention and Sexuality Education Must Change to Meet Their Promise," *SIECUS Report*, vol. 31, October/November 2002, p. 5. Copyright © 2002 by Sexuality Information and Education Council of the U.S., Inc. Reproduced by permission.

All over the world, education is identified as having a critical role to play in teaching people about sex, sexuality, and the prevention of HIV/AIDS. Yet all too often, the radical potential of education to promote safer and more pleasurable kinds of sex and to effect change remains unfulfilled.

In study after study, for example, young people state that what education they have received about HIV/AIDS was "too little, too late," and substantial numbers of adults continue to have serious misconceptions about the epidemic. These range from the view expressed in a recent Australian study of young heterosexual men that HIV/AIDS is a disease of "dirty women and gay men" to the continued belief among large numbers of adults in developing countries that condoms have holes through which HIV can pass. Clearly, in many ways, education is failing to live up to its potential—and we as educators must bear some of the responsibility for this.

I want to address some of the issues upon which education must focus if it is to fulfill its promise in HIV/AIDS prevention and care. There has never been a better moment for this. A new strategic framework for such education to which the United Nations Education, Scientific, and Cultural Organization (UNESCO) and all other cosponsors from the Joint United Nations Programme on HIV/AIDS (UNAIDS) have signed, is currently being finalized. This offers an excellent starting point for more explicit and coordinated efforts.

The Focus of AIDS Education

It should go without saying that much HIV/AIDS education has focused heavily upon knowledge, attitudes, and behaviors. Both adults and young people have been taught the "facts" in the belief that they will then act on the basis of what they know.

Alternatively, they have been given the chance to reflect on existing attitudes they may hold or others around them may hold—attitudes toward sexual practices, for example.

Beyond this, there has been an emphasis on skills acquisition—so-called "life skills" related to decision making as well as skills of sexual "communication" and "negotiation."

But too often, the focus is on the isolated individual who

must be "taught," who must learn the "right attitudes," and who must become "skilled." Rarely, if ever, has there been concern about the affective and emotional—what people feel about the issues as well as what they know and do.

All of us probably know that our judgement about sexual and drug-related matters can be swayed by circumstance. And if this is true for us, then it must be true for others.

But why is this true? At least part of the answer is found in the different meanings that operate within a given context. What sex or drug use signifies, for example, can influence whether or not someone engages in it. And meanings shift and change depending on circumstances.

Notions of honor, for example, are central to sexual self-understanding. For many young men and some young women, it is "honorable" to show that they are sexually experienced. For many young people involved in sex work in countries such as Thailand, it is "honorable" to send earned money to parents in the village. For many of us, it is "honorable" to remain faithful to our sexual partners. But these "honors" differ according to context and circumstance.

The Power of Irrationality

It is also important to recognize irrationality as a powerful force structuring sexual life. Rarely are the kinds of interaction that lead to sex best understood in terms of the negotiation and communication taught in "Just Say No" programs.

Rarely does one weigh all the pros and cons of having sex in the ways suggested by rational decision-making models of risk-related behavior and behavior change. While actions can be re-constructed in this way after the event, at the time they are more often than not responses to opportunity and chance.

The power of transgression—or the excitement that comes from doing something unusual or naughty, that is forbidden—is, I believe, also underestimated. True, there has been talk about such issues within the context of some gay men's apparent abandonment of condoms and the adoption of new and more complex forms of negotiated safety. But there has been relatively little attention given to transgression within heterosexual "safer sex" education or drug-use education.

Finally, there is the thorny issue of love, a concept conspicuous by its absence on the agendas of many conferences dealing with sexuality-related issues. While concepts of love vary considerably around the world, they are real enough for many people (at least some of the time).

As François Delor's recent work on sero-discordant couples in France shows, love legitimizes a range of sexual practices where the likelihood of HIV transmission is very real— unsafe sex between long-established sero-discordant partners, for example, who believe that the passions of first encounters will last.

We are left, therefore, with a series of important absences in the focus of much education relating to HIV/AIDS.

The Range of Matters Addressed

The absence of certain subjects in education is compounded by what might be called a series of approaches to such education that have solidified over the years. I will say something about five.

First, until recently, the majority of general population or school-based *HIV/AIDS* education initiatives have proceeded from the erroneous belief that all of those whom educators are trying to reach are HIV negative. This is dangerous not only because the majority of individuals simply do not know their sero status but also because, in an increasing number of circumstances (and most certainly within schools throughout Africa), a substantial proportion of both teachers and pupils may be (and may know themselves to be) HIV positive. The barriers between primary prevention and other forms of prevention are breaking down.

Second, and not unrelated to the above, is the erroneous belief that people with HIV/AIDS are some kind of a problem and not part of the solution to the epidemic. Frightening imagery of the physical effects of HIV/AIDS, together with warnings to young people to avoid those who might pose a "risk" do little to build the kinds of social solidarity central to an effective response. In contexts where relatively few people know their sero status, this assumption reinforces denial, making the educated "take sides" in a divisive and unnecessary battle against the epidemic.

Third, AIDS education programs are among the rela-

116

tively few educational programs to date where stigma, discrimination, and human rights are central to prevention work. It is a sad fact that it has taken nearly 20 years for the first World AIDS Campaign to focus on what arguably is the greatest social ill associated with the epidemic: namely, the willingness of people to ostracize, vilify, and reject their brothers and sisters, sons and daughters, friends and lovers. HIV/AIDS education needs to get real in addressing these elements of social abuse.

Anderson. © 1992 by Kirk Anderson. Reproduced by permission.

Fourth, until recently our understanding of gender has been relatively superficial in our educational work. True, it cannot be denied that women, and young women in particular, are systematically disadvantaged in the majority of the world's societies. And true, for many young women, education represents a route out of poverty and away from sexual health risk. Having said this, and as Dr. Geeta Rao Gupta of the International Center for Research on Women in Washington, DC, has pointed out in the last two international HIV/AIDS conferences, we have failed to engage adequately with the manner in which gender systems work to ensure that both women and men are rendered vulnerable to the epidemic:

Men, through ideologies that encourage them to appear knowledgeable when they are not (for fear of threatening their manhood); women, through ideologies that encourage them to be "innocent" about sex when they need to know.

Fifth, there has been the belief that the messages and approaches that worked early on in the AIDS epidemic will continue to do so. Nothing could be further from the truth. It is now abundantly clear from research with some of the first groups known to be infected (gay men, sex workers, and injecting drugs users) that messages and approaches have to be changed over time. Not only are new generations of especially vulnerable people always in the making, but they enter into this world in circumstances very different from those that prevailed early in the epidemic, when any talk of effective treatment was nothing short of a fantasy.

The Issue of Pedagogy

Too often, HIV/AIDS education has proceeded from what Professor Richard Parker of Columbia University and I have called a model of "liberal enlightenment." Here, those who know best intervene to correct the "bad" thoughts and actions of others.

This "banking" theory of pedagogy, as the educator Paulo Freire once described it, sees the minds of those who are being educated as empty vessels waiting to be filled with the good ideas of intervention specialists and communications experts.

A parallel set of assumptions leads us to understand sex as a behavior to be controlled, not a passion to be played with safely. Needless to say, people are rarely taken in by such formal pedagogic approaches. More often than not, they end up paying lip service. They may appear to listen carefully but change little behind the scenes.

More successful by far are efforts to unleash the power of critical and systematic thought based on people's own positions in life. Such approaches usually have their starting point in the everyday concerns of individuals, not in those of intervention experts and specialists.

It is this kind of pedagogy that has characterized, at various times and in disparate ways, the prevention work of programs and projects as diverse as the Sonagachi project working with female sex workers in India, TASO (The AIDS Service Organization) working with a wide range of individuals in Uganda, the Gay Men's Health Crisis (GMHC) in New York City, the various AIDS Councils in Australia, and Grupo PelaVidda in Brazil.

In each case, the principal aim of the pedagogy was not to tell people what to do but to unleash the power of community to take charge and fight back. The importance of such approaches—which seek to consolidate and build social capital—is well documented, especially in contexts where "popular education" was used to help develop nor only understanding but also to combat the social inequality and exclusion that disempowers those most vulnerable to HIV.

The Issue of Context

Perhaps the most important thing to take into account in planning future work relating to AIDS education is the notion of context. Far from being peripheral to the effectiveness of education, context the "background noise"—is vitally important to understanding how people respond to learning opportunities.

Let me give you an example. It might matter enormously what we should do to promote safer sex in an educational setting if that sex is: (1) first sex or regular sex, (2) sex within an enduring marital relationship or sex on an occasional basis outside this relationship, (3) sex with love or sex in order to satisfy a momentary feeling of lust, (4) sex freely entered into by consenting adults or sex within the context of "ethnic cleansing," or (5) the sex that occurs between men in prisons or the sex that takes place in loving gay relationships.

Ultimately, there are no universal panaceas to discover in prevention science. The approaches we use must be context specific. Context matters when it comes to planning interventions and thinking about what education can achieve.

Context is important because of its intimate relationship with what we call vulnerability. Undertaking HIV/AIDS prevention requires focusing not only on individual risk-taking behavior but also on the environmental, political, and economic factors that influence susceptibility or vulnerability.

We need to take into account key sets of variables: factors linked to social networks and relationships, factors pertaining to the quality and coverage of services and programs, and broad-based societal factors. . . .

Some 20 years into the global HIV/AIDS epidemic, the time is ripe to re-evaluate what counts as HIV/AIDS education. New and more realistic programs and interventions are needed if we are ever to meet the goals set out in the Declaration of Commitment of the United Nations General Assembly Special Session on HIV/AIDS (UNGASS).

Business as usual will not work. We need to radically renew and upgrade our efforts if the potential of education to change lives and to promote reductions in HIV/AIDS related vulnerability and risk is to be fully realized.

Periodical Bibliography

The following articles have been selected to supplement the diverse views presented in this chapter.

Alexandra Arriaga	"HIV/AIDS and Violence Against Women," *Human Rights*, Summer 2002.
Albert-Laszlo Barabasi	"To Combat AIDS, Help the Few to Save the Many," *Los Angeles Times*, May 21, 2002.
Salih Booker	"Last in Line: Africa Doesn't Rate in U.S. Foreign Relations," *Crisis* (NAACP), May/June 2003.
Holly Burkhalter	"The Politics of AIDS," *Foreign Affairs*, January/February 2004.
Marilyn Chase	"Noted Researcher Retracts Key Finding on AIDS Immunity," *Wall Street Journal*, January 23, 2004.
Church & State	"Religious Right Leaders Seek to Hijack Overseas AIDS Prevention Effort," April 2003.
Charles Colson	"Beyond Condoms: To Alleviate AIDS, We Must Sharpen Our Moral Vision," *Christianity Today*, June 2003.
David Ehrenstein	"The 10 Biggest Lies About AIDS," *Advocate*, April 1, 2003.
Tom Farley	"Cruise Control: Bathhouses Are Reigniting the AIDS Crisis. It's Time to Shut Them Down," *Washington Monthly*, November 2002.
Edward C. Green	"Culture Clash and AIDS Prevention," *Responsive Community*, Fall 2003.
Daniel Judy	"Teens Need More Information About AIDS," *SIECUS Report*, April/May 2003.
Alison Katz	"AIDS in Africa," *Z Magazine*, September 2003.
Nicholas D. Kristof	"The Secret War on Condoms," *New York Times*, January 10, 2003.
Rene Sanchez	"An AIDS Reality Check," *Washington Post National Weekly Edition*, May 20–26, 2002.
Elizabeth Terzakis	"Global AIDS Catastrophe," *International Socialist Review*, September/October 2002.
Virus Weekly	"Drugs Can Eradicate AIDS Epidemic," August 27, 2002.

CHAPTER 3

Are Vaccines Harmful?

Chapter Preface

Mary Clayton-Enderlein became concerned when one of her son's regularly visiting playmates developed an unusual cough: a high-pitched "whoop" while gasping for air. The playmate's mother admitted that he might have contracted whooping cough, as their family did not believe in vaccinations. One week later, Enderlein herself came down with whooping cough just before giving birth to her second son, Colin. The newborn also became ill—turning blue as repeated coughing spells racked his body. The baby spent ten days in an intensive-care unit, and Enderlein, Colin, and the child who infected them did not fully recover for months.

Despite the obvious success that vaccines have had in decreasing the occurrence of infectious childhood diseases, a small but growing number of parents are reluctant to immunize their children. Recent reports connecting vaccines with life-threatening adverse reactions and chronic disorders such as asthma, autism, immune system dysfunction, and mental retardation have prompted some families to opt out of government-promoted childhood immunization programs. Most physicians and public health experts are troubled by this trend. They maintain that critics have greatly exaggerated the risks of immunization and argue that the benefits of vaccines greatly exceed their potential dangers.

Much of the effectiveness of vaccines, health experts point out, is due to "herd immunity," a resistance to epidemics that occurs when at least 90 percent of the population has been vaccinated. As the number of people avoiding vaccination increases, the strength of herd immunity decreases. "Because vaccines protect both the individual and the community, decisions about opting out of immunizations have both personal and community implications," explains Bruce Gellin, executive director of the National Immunization Information Network. He compares the concept of herd immunity to a four-way stop sign: "A person who decides to ignore the stop sign knows he has less risk of an accident if others obey it. However, if two drivers make a similar decision, assuming that the other will stop, the outcome becomes much more risky for everyone in the intersection."

And as Mary Clayton-Enderlein's experience shows, it is not only one unvaccinated child who is endangered by illness but also those he comes in contact with—particularly people with weakened immune systems, such as the elderly, the pregnant, and the newborn.

Many immunization critics, on the other hand, state that they are not anti-vaccine but believe that more research is needed to investigate the possible connection between vaccinations and chronic disorders. "Instead of epidemics of measles and polio, we have epidemics of chronic autoimmune and neurological disease," says Barbara Loe Fisher, cofounder of the National Vaccines Information Center. Fisher and her supporters claim that children with a family history of immune system disorders or other genetic vulnerabilities are more likely to experience severe vaccine reactions that could result in developmental disabilities or chronic illnesses. Vaccination critics maintain that these children should not be subjected to a "one size fits all" immunization policy—an approach that ignores individual differences to fulfill public health requirements. Parents should instead be fully informed of the risks and allowed to exempt their children from vaccination programs when necessary, explains Fisher.

The controversy over immunizations and vaccine safety presents an interesting quandary: Those who avoid vaccines because they may be sensitive to side effects must rely on herd immunity to protect them from illness, yet the growing population of the unvaccinated itself poses a threat to herd immunity. In the following chapter authors continue this discussion on the benefits and risks of vaccination.

"[It is irresponsible] to assume that there is no connection between the ever increasing numbers of vaccines we mandate . . . and the ever increasing rates of chronic disease in our children."

Mandating Vaccination Is Harmful

Barbara Loe Fisher

Vaccines can be a causal factor in chronic health problems such as asthma, diabetes, attention deficit disorder, and autism, contends Barbara Loe Fisher in the following viewpoint. The medical community, however, denies the potential risks of vaccination even though chronic illnesses have become more prevalent as the number of mandated childhood vaccines has increased. Moreover, Fisher points out, safety tests on new vaccines are rife with methodological flaws and statistical errors. Rather than requiring all children to be vaccinated, parents should be fully informed of the merits and risks of vaccines and be allowed to opt out of immunization programs if they believe their children would be endangered. Fisher is the cofounder and president of the National Vaccine Information Center.

As you read, consider the following questions:
1. By what percentage have attention deficit disorder and asthma increased over the past two decades, according to the author?
2. In what ways were the clinical trials of the experimental Prevnar vaccine flawed, in Fisher's opinion?

Barbara Loe Fisher, testimony before the California Senate Committee on Health and Human Services, Sacramento, CA, January 23, 2002.

Editor's Note: This viewpoint is excerpted from Fisher's January 2002 testimony before the California Senate Committee on Health and Human Services.

I am appearing here on behalf of the 4,500 California parent and health professional members of the National Vaccine Information Center, which is a 40,000-member national, nonprofit organization founded in 1982 by parents of vaccine injured children. My organization worked with Congress in the 1980's to create the National Childhood Vaccine Injury Act of 1986 and we were instrumental in helping to obtain the safer DTaP [diphtheria/tetanus/pertussis] vaccine licensed in 1996 for America's babies. Our mission is to prevent vaccine injuries and deaths through public education and we support the availability of vaccines for all who want to use them but we also endorse the ethical principle of informed consent and believe that the zealous enforcement of vaccine mandates threaten that principle.

My 20-year experience as a vaccine safety consumer advocate includes co-authorship of the 1985 book *DPT: A Shot in the Dark*, which was used as a reference by the Institute of Medicine in its historic reports on vaccine adverse events in 1991 and 1994, as well as appointments to the National Vaccine Advisory Committee in 1988 and the Institute of Medicine Vaccine Safety Forum in 1995. I am currently the consumer voting member of the FDA [Food and Drug Administration] Vaccines and Related Biological Products Advisory Committee.

Vaccine Injured Children

Personally, I come here as a parent of a son who had a neurological reaction to his fourth DPT shot at age two and a half that caused brain dysfunction, including multiple learning disabilities and attention deficit disorder (ADD), but who was fortunate not to lose his life or be left with mental retardation, uncontrolled epilepsy, autism, or other severe disabilities like so many of the vaccine injured children I have come to know. When my son had his vaccine reaction in 1980, children in America were told to get 23 doses of 7 vaccines. Today, children are told to get 37 doses of 11 vaccines. In those 22 years since my son had his vaccine reaction, the numbers of American children with learning disabilities, attention deficit disorder and asthma have doubled; diabetes has tripled; and the incidence of autism has reached epidemic proportions, increasing 200 to 600 percent in every state, marking a staggering 3400 percent increase in the prevalence of autism in our children.

Nobody knows why this has happened. But everyone at the Centers for Disease Control [CDC] and American Academy of Pediatrics, the two medical groups that make vaccine policy in this country, vigorously deny that the many vaccines they have urged be mandated in the past quarter century could have anything to do with why more and more of our children are chronically ill. They say that vaccines only rarely cause chronic health problems.

Yet, the haunting question remains: if we have wiped out polio and almost eliminated measles, mumps, rubella, whooping cough and other childhood diseases with vaccines—why are so many of our children stuck on sick? Why are our special education classrooms so crowded that we can't find enough money or train teachers fast enough to care for these learning disabled, hyperactive, autistic, asthmatic, diabetic, emotionally disturbed, sick children?

Something is wrong with this public health report card.

The Need for Research

And before we go any further and mandate one more vaccine for daycare or kindergarten entry—whether it is Prevnar or hepatitis A or some other vaccine—we had better find out if the repeated manipulation of the immune system with lab altered viruses and bacteria adulterated with mercury, aluminum, formaldehyde and other toxins, which are administered to our babies from birth through the first five years of life when the brain and immune system is developing at its most rapid rate, is contributing to these skyrocketing increases in chronic illness in our children. Without basic science research into the biological mechanisms of vaccine injury and death and without methodologically sound, long-term studies which follow groups of highly vaccinated, lesser vaccinated and unvaccinated children over time to measure for all morbidity and mortality outcomes, it is illogical and scientifically irresponsible to assume that there is no connection between the ever increasing numbers of vaccines we mandate for children and the ever increasing rates of chronic disease in our children. Making this kind of scientific investigation a societal program and funding priority would, at the very least, give us a better understanding of the genetic and other biological factors which predispose certain children to vaccine-induced immune and brain dysfunction, including whether there is a complex interaction between genetic factors, a particular vaccine or combination of vaccines and simultaneous exposures to environmental contaminants such as pesticides, molds and other toxic insults.

I understand that you are looking at whether the process for mandating childhood vaccines in California could be improved. You have a difficult job to do because when you make laws, you often rely upon expert advice in areas where you don't feel you have enough expertise. Medicine is an area that a lot of us feel like we don't have the knowledge or expertise to make independent decisions.

As a mother who graduated from college but never went to medical school or got a Ph.D., I urge you not to totally defer to the experts on this one. You are smart or you wouldn't have been elected. As legislators, you educate yourselves about everything from freeway construction to pollution to the death penalty. Those are complex issues just like this one—and it doesn't take a medical degree to tell the difference between a good scientific study and a bad one.

Investigative Flaws

I voted "NO" when I was asked in 1999, as the consumer member of an FDA Committee, to vote on whether Wyeth Lederle, the manufacturer of Prevnar, had proved the vaccine is safe. I was the only "no" vote, but I voted "no" with confidence. I remembered being taught in a high school science class that when correctly employing the scientific method to prove an hypothesis in an experiment, you cannot compare two unknowns. The Prevnar pre-licensure clinical trials, which Wyeth Lederle paid Kaiser Permanente to conduct, compared two experimental vaccines against each other. To compound this basic methodological flaw, Kaiser and Wyeth Lederle, allowed most of the children in the trial to be given the more reactive DPT vaccine rather than use the safer, less reactive DTaP vaccine. This placed the children in that five-year experiment in greater danger and allowed the drug company to write off the seizures that occurred as being caused by DPT and not Prevnar, when in fact, they didn't know. Even so, the groups of children who got Prevnar suffered more seizures, higher fevers, more irritability and other reactions than did the children who got the other experimental vaccine. It was a no-brainer as far as I was concerned: Kaiser and Wyeth Lederle had proved nothing about Prevnar vaccine safety.

Questioning Mandatory Immunization

Decades of studies published in the world's leading medical journals have documented vaccine failure and serious adverse vaccine events, including death. Dozens of books written by doctors, researchers, and independent investigators reveal serious flaws in immunization theory and practice. Yet, incredibly, most pediatricians and parents are unaware of these findings. This has begun to change in recent years, however, as a growing number of parents and healthcare providers around the world are becoming aware of the problems and questioning mass mandatory immunization. *There is a growing international movement away from mass mandatory immunization.*

Alan Phillips, www.unc.edu, April 1998.

And another question: why did the CDC's policymaking committee vote to recommend "universal use" of Prevnar by all children *before* the FDA Committee even got a chance to review the data and take a vote about whether it should be licensed at all? The same thing happened with the ill-fated Rotavirus vaccine for infant diarrhea that was pulled off the market in 1999, less than a year after it was released, because it was causing bowel obstructions in babies. The CDC had voted to recommend that all babies get rotavirus vaccine weeks before the FDA Committee voted on scientific proof of safety and efficacy. And before the FDA Committee even got a chance to vote on Prevnar, Wyeth Lederle and Kaiser

Permanente officials were being quoted in national press releases that Prevnar was an ear infection vaccine—when their own trial data showed that the vaccine only decreased a child's chance of getting an ear infection by 7 percent!

The FDA has never licensed Prevnar as an ear infection vaccine but lots of doctors in America tell parents it is because that is how the vaccine has been promoted. No wonder Prevnar vaccine was the number one best selling new pharmaceutical introduced to the market in the year 2000—generating more than $450 million for Wyeth Lederle that year.

Conflicts of Interest

Which brings us to the uncomfortable issue of conflicts of interest that exist when experts, who sit on vaccine advisory committees, also get paid by vaccine manufacturers to conduct clinical trials on vaccines they make and sell. It happens too often and it contributes to the erosion of trust in the integrity of a mass vaccination system where the same doctors, who report parents to child social services for child abuse if the parent doesn't want the child vaccinated with every mandated vaccine, are the same doctors who refuse to obey the 1986 law and report injuries and deaths following vaccination to the federal Vaccine Adverse Event Reporting System (VAERS). The estimate is that less than 10 percent, perhaps less than one percent, of all doctors report serious health problems that follow vaccination. So instead of the some 12,000 reports that are made every year, there may be as many as 120,000 to 1.2 million vaccine-related adverse events occurring annually that nobody is counting or following up on. And this means that the more than 3,000 Prevnar vaccine adverse events that have been reported to VAERS since 2000 and the more than 2,500 hepatitis A vaccine adverse events that have been reported since 1996 are only a fraction of what has really occurred.

The truth is we really don't know how many children are getting seriously ill and dying following vaccination in America every year. Doctors and public health officials, anxious to persuade themselves and the public that vaccine risks are minimal, use the remarkably unscientific argument that it is all a "coincidence" when something bad happens to a child after vaccination—the vaccine is never, ever to blame. And so more and more parents, who took a bright, healthy, normally developing child to a doctor's office for routine vaccinations, are coming forward with their dead and damaged children asking you to fix a mass vaccination system they know is broken.

I urge you not be afraid to rely on your intelligence and common sense to evaluate the merits, potential risks, and very real costs associated with mandating new vaccines such as Prevnar and hepatitis A. There are more than 200 experimental vaccines being developed to prevent everything from tooth decay to stomach ulcers, as well as a supervaccine to be given at birth that will inject raw DNA from 20 to 30 different viruses and bacteria directly into the cells of newborns. The vaccine manufacturers and physician special interest groups that will lobby you for mandates know that drug companies and doctors have been protected from liability for vaccine injuries and deaths since the 1986 vaccine injury compensation law was passed. I worked with Congress in the early 1980's on that law and have watched it be turned into a cruel joke as 2 out of 3 vaccine injured children are denied federal compensation for their often catastrophic vaccine injuries because the DHHS [Department of Health and Human Services] and the Department of Justice officials fight every claim, viewing every award to a vaccine injured child as admission that vaccines can and do cause harm.

The Violation of Informed Consent

Please remember that when you mandate, rather than recommend, a medical procedure like vaccination that carries a risk of injury or death, it sets the stage for violation of informed consent, an ethical standard that has guided the practice of medicine since World War II. One of the reasons I traveled from Virginia to be here today is to defend the human right to informed consent which is embodied in the religious and personal or conscientious belief exemption to vaccination now protected in California law. In many other states, public health and education officials are determined to eliminate these exemptions from the law. We have examples of parents in Wyoming, New York and other states being detained by state government officials and interrogated for hours about the sincerity of their deeply held religious or conscientious beliefs only to find their previously held exemptions revoked; their children barred from attending school and a threat that their child will be taken away from them.

Those exemptions are the closest we come in America to preventing the unchecked implementation of utilitarianism, which attempts to justify the forced sacrifice of some in service to others. There is nothing that causes a crisis of trust in government more than when the people live in fear of a law that forces them to risk their lives or the lives of their children without their consent. I hope that this Committee, in considering any new vaccine mandates or other laws which force vaccination—even in times of emergency—will protect the inviolability of the informed consent ethic which, at its most basic level, respects the right of the individual to voluntarily decide what he or she is willing to die for.

"When vaccination rates drop, disease returns."

Avoiding Vaccination Is Harmful

Arthur Allen

In recent years a growing number of parents and medical establishment critics have raised concerns about the safety of vaccines and have expressed opposition to state regulations that make vaccinations a mandatory condition for school enrollment. In the following viewpoint Arthur Allen contends that there is no evidence of a causal relationship between vaccines and conditions such as asthma, autism, or multiple sclerosis. He also maintains that parents who refuse to have their children vaccinated are putting entire communities at risk for outbreaks of disease. In Colorado, for example—a state where parents can exempt their children from immunization—whooping cough is on the rise, writes Allen. Allen is a Washington, D.C.–based freelance journalist who frequently writes on medical matters.

As you read, consider the following questions:
1. What percentage of parents has reservations about vaccines, according to Allen?
2. In what way is immunization "a victim of its own success," in the author's opinion?
3. According to Allen, how many U.S. cases of whooping cough were there in 1994? In 2001?

Boulder, Colorado, a university town of 96,000, lies in a sequestered valley on the western edge of the Great Plains. Both geographically and culturally it is a place apart. [Consumer advocate and Green Party candidate] Ralph Nader won more than 10 percent of Boulder's vote in the [2000] presidential election. Natural-food groceries outnumber Safeways; chiropractors' offices line the main drag; and the city council recently declared that dog owners would henceforth be referred to as "dog guardians." A popular bumper sticker reads, WELCOME TO BOULDER, 20 SQUARE MILES SURROUNDED BY REALITY. Boulder is, in short, an experiment-oriented city.

A particularly interesting experiment, from a public-health perspective, has taken shape at the Shining Mountain Waldorf School, a campus of one-story wooden buildings set amid cottonwood and willow trees by the foothills of the Rockies. By their parents' choosing, nearly half of the 292 students at Shining Mountain have received only a few, and in some cases none, of the twenty-one childhood vaccinations mandated by Colorado state law in accordance with federal guidelines. The shunning of one of the vaccines, against diphtheria, tetanus, and pertussis, has resulted in a revival of whooping cough, the illness that occurs when colonies of the bacteria Bordetella pertussis attach to the lining of the upper respiratory passages, releasing toxins that cause inflammation and a spasmodic cough. The high-pitched whoop is a symptom heard mainly in younger children; it's the sound of a desperate attempt to breathe.

Shining Mountain exemplifies a growing movement in American life: the challenge to childhood vaccination. According to a survey published in the November 2000 issue of *Pediatrics*, one fourth of all parents are skeptical of some or all of the standard vaccines. Some states grant exemptions to the law so that parents can refuse vaccinations for their children. In Colorado parents who don't want their children vaccinated have only to sign a card stating as much. In Oregon the rate of religious exemption—which are granted to all parents who choose not to have their children immunized for philosophical reasons—tripled, from 0.9 percent in the 1996–1997 school year to 2.7 percent in 2001.

Those skeptical of vaccines have various reasons. Some believe that vaccines are responsible for otherwise unexplained increases in conditions such as autism, asthma, and multiple sclerosis. Others, including the conservative activist Phyllis Schlafly, see government attempts to track and enforce immunization as an intrusion on privacy. Still others—parents whose recollections of their own bouts of chickenpox or measles are bathed in nostalgia—argue that the elimination of traditional childhood illnesses is an attack on childhood itself. The parents at Shining Mountain are influenced by the philosophy of Rudolf Steiner, a turn-of-the-century Austrian philosopher who founded the Waldorf movement. Steiner (who was not a medical doctor) believed that children's spirits benefited from being tempered in the fires of a good inflammation.

The critics have concluded that the dangers of vaccination outweigh the risks of vaccine-preventable disease. Like all medical interventions, vaccination entails some risk, although the extent and gravity of potential side effects are matters of debate. For example, febrile seizures occur in roughly one in 10,000 children—perhaps 1,000 a year in the United States—who receive the current whooping-cough vaccine. Such seizures rarely, if ever, lead to permanent brain damage, however, and in any case febrile seizures are triggered just as easily by a run-of-the-mill infection as by a vaccine. Suspicions that mercury preservatives used in vaccines inflicted neurological damage on children are worrisome but unproved (mercury has largely been phased out of vaccines over the past three years).

A Victim of Success

To some extent vaccination is a victim of its own success. Owing to vaccination campaigns, smallpox no longer exists in man, and polio has been driven from the Western Hemisphere. Measles, diphtheria, and invasive hemophilus bacterial disease (such as meningitis) are rare in the United States, and even whooping cough is unusual enough that few parents consider it a threat. All these diseases, with the exception of smallpox, still infest various corners of the world, but in most of the United States even those who have not been vaccinated against them, or in whom the vaccine is not effective, are protected, because most of the people we meet have been vaccinated. Epidemiologists call this phenomenon "herd immunity": the more vaccinated sheep there are, the safer an unvaccinated one is. When vaccination rates drop, disease returns.

The History of Measles

1958–1962: Over a half a million cases of measles are reported each year. 432 measles-related deaths occur on average each year.

Measles vaccine is licensed.

By 2000, only 81 cases are reported in all of the U.S.!

| 1958 | 1962 | 1963 | 2000 |

Centers for Disease Control and Prevention, www.cdc.gov, no date.

Precisely at what point herd immunity fails is difficult to calculate, but there is ample evidence that it does. Since the collapse of the Soviet public-health system diphtheria has returned to Russia with a vengeance, killing thousands. Sweden suspended vaccination against whooping cough from 1979 to 1996 while testing a new vaccine. In a study of the moratorium period that was published in 1993, Swedish physicians found that 60 percent of the country's children got whooping cough before they were ten. However, close medical monitoring kept the death rate from whooping cough at about one per year during that period.

Boulder, which has the lowest schoolwide vaccination rate in Colorado, has one of the highest per capita rates of whooping cough in the United States. The problem started in 1993, when fifty-two people in Boulder County contracted the disease. Since then the county has seen an average of eighty-one cases a year. Although unvaccinated children are six times as likely as vaccinated children to get whooping cough during an outbreak, about half the cases in Colorado have involved vaccinated children; the whooping-cough vaccine sometimes fails to produce effective immunity, and even successful pertussis immunity generally wanes by age ten. "At first we called it an outbreak; then we started calling it a sustained outbreak, now we just say it's endemic," Ann Marie Bailey, the county nurse epidemiologist when I visited Boulder [in 2001], told me.

To many in Boulder, endemic pertussis is no cause for alarm. Shining Mountain's director, Robert Schiappacasse, says that his daughter, who had been immunized, got whooping cough but suffered no lasting effects. He became a little concerned, he told me, when the baby of one of the school's secretaries "coughed himself into a hernia" after visiting the school during an outbreak. Still, "parents here" Schiappacasse said, apparently including himself in the category, "are more likely to be worried about fumes from a new carpet than they are about any infectious disease."

I also spoke with Johnnie Egars, a Shining Mountain parent whose three children, all unvaccinated, got whooping cough in 1994. Her youngest child was particularly sick. Egars's description of the experience was harrowing. "It was a loud cough that went down to her toes, and the whoop was a sharp intake of breath" she recalled. "She coughed and coughed until she threw up, then she slept an hour or two. Then she'd wake up and start over again." The daughter, who was two at the time, was undergoing treatment for cancer; she was hospitalized for three days in the infectious-diseases ward of Children's Hospital in Denver. Nonetheless, Egars is comfortable with her decision not to vaccinate her children. A niece was hospitalized with febrile seizures following a pertussis vaccination, and in her view, "immunization just weakens the immune system." She adds, "We have a history of cancer in my family, so we try to do everything we can to strengthen the immune system."

From its reservoir in the undervaccinated population of Boulder pertussis has branched out: neighboring Jefferson and Denver Counties had more cases in 2000 than Boulder did. Some of the people who live near Boulder are angry. "There is a constant presence of whooping cough here, and it's because of Boulder Valley," says Kathy Keffeler, the chief school nurse for Longmont, a growing city just north of Boulder.

Pertussis is on the rise not just in Colorado but across the country: there were 7,600 cases [in 2001], as compared with 4,600 in 1994. It can be fatal, especially in countries—like ours—with spotty health-care coverage. In 2000 it killed seventeen people in the United States, including two Colorado babies, both of whom were taken to the hospital too late. "It was very sad," Tina Albertson, a pediatric resident who cared for one of the infants, told me. "She was a six-week-old girl with a sister and a brother, four and six. The family had chosen not to immunize, and the week she was born, her siblings both had whooping cough. When they're real little, the babies don't whoop—they just stop breathing. This little girl was septic by the time they got her here."

Like most in Boulder, Ann Marie Bailey, the nurse epidemiologist, is tolerant of the alternative healthcare scene; she cedes nonvaccinating parents the right to decide what's best for their children. But she gently points out that they're fooling themselves if they think no one else is affected by their decisions. "We've been able to show very definitely that whooping cough spreads from these pockets in small communities. If they lived in a vacuum at Shining Mountain—if they never went out to go swimming or to church or the YMCA or the Boy Scouts—it would be a different ball game," she told me.

Jia Gottlieb, a family practitioner who offers acupuncture and breathing exercises along with traditional medicine, said, "When I get parents who don't vaccinate, I tell them, 'When your boy gets a vaccination he takes on a risk for the public good, just like the firemen [at the World Trade Center] who went back into the buildings.'" But Gottlieb's words usually fall on deaf ears. "These are probably people who donate a lot of money to good causes," he said, "but their view is 'I'm going to let everyone else's child take a risk but not my own?' That's not avant-garde. That's not enlightened. It's pretty primitive. And ironically, in a town like Boulder the selfish strategy is probably not in the best interests of your child either."

"For years there has been a debate about the cause or causes of autism, but the vast majority of finger-pointing has been directed at childhood vaccines."

Vaccines May Cause Autism

Kelly Patricia O'Meara

Vaccines containing thimerosal, a mercury-containing preservative, are likely the cause of the recent surge in autism cases in the United States, reports Kelly Patricia O'Meara in the following viewpoint. The incidence of autism—a once-rare illness— has increased by at least 500 percent since 1992, she points out. A recent study indicates that American infants have been exposed to excessive amounts of mercury through vaccines, and that toxic levels of mercury can result in neurodevelopment disorders such as autism. Although public health officials claim that thimerosal has now been removed from vaccines, labels and package inserts reveal that some vaccines still contain mercury. O'Meara is an investigative reporter for *Insight on the News*, a national biweekly newsmagazine.

As you read, consider the following questions:
1. By how much did the rate of California children diagnosed with autism increase between 1999 and 2002, according to O'Meara?
2. What are some of the substances contained in vaccines, according to the author?
3. In the opinion of Mark Geier, quoted by the author, why have pharmaceutical companies not yet removed mercury from all vaccines?

The mother of an autistic child wonders aloud when health officials will wake up to the epidemic that has claimed not only her son but hundreds of thousands of other children in the United States, with no end in sight. She muses, "Maybe someday this will be as important as SARS [Severe Acute Respiratory Syndrome] and we'll get the same attention. God knows we need it."

Autism is a severely incapacitating developmental disability for which there is no known cure. According to a recently released report by the California Department of Developmental Services (DDS) entitled Autistic Spectrum Disorders, Changes in the California Caseload: 1999–2002, the rate of children diagnosed with full-syndrome autism in the Golden State between 1999 and 2002 nearly doubled from 10,360 to 20,377. The report further revealed that "between Dec. 31, 1987, and Dec. 31, 2002, the population of persons with full-syndrome autism has increased by 634 percent." That is a doubling of autism cases every four years, and the staggering increases are not limited to California.

Skyrocketing Autism Rates

According to data provided by the U.S. Department of Education, the increased autism rate in California is in line with the increases other states are experiencing. For example, in 1992 Ohio reported 22 cases. A decade later the number had increased by 13,895 percent to 3,057. In Illinois the rate of autism cases climbed from just five in 1992 to 3,802 an increase of 76,040 percent. Mississippi, New Hampshire and the District of Columbia reported no cases of autism in 1992, but by 2002 the number of cases reported were 461,404 and 144, respectively. Only Puerto Rico can claim to have an increase of less than 100 percent, with the remaining states reporting increases of at least 500 percent during the same period.

Although once considered rare, during the last two decades the chance of a child being diagnosed with autism has skyrocketed from one in 10,000 to one in 150. In California, full-syndrome autism now is the No. 1 disability among children and more prevalent than childhood cancer, diabetes and Down's syndrome. It is estimated that [by 2007] autism cases in the Golden State will exceed the total number of cases of both cerebral palsy and epilepsy. To get a better idea of how quickly the epidemic is spreading one need only consider that in 1987 there were 2,778 persons with autism in California. By 2002 the number had increased to 20,377, and in 2002 3,575 new cases had been added to the rolls, far exceeding the total number of cases in the state 15 years earlier.

For years there has been a debate about the cause or causes of autism, but the vast majority of finger-pointing has been directed at childhood vaccines as the culprit. And considering what is put into the vaccines injected into hours-old infants, it is easy to understand why they are at the top of the list of suspects: formaldehyde (used in embalming), thimerosal (nearly 50 percent mercury), aluminum phosphate (toxic and carcinogenic), antibiotics, phenols (corrosive to skin and toxic), aluminum salts (corrosive to tissue and neurotoxic), methanol (toxic), isopropyl (toxic), 2-pheoxyethanol (toxic), live viruses and a host of unknown components considered off-limits as trade secrets. These are just part of the vaccine mixture.

The Dangers of Thimerosal

For those who believe there are elements in vaccines that may be responsible for the increased number of autism cases and other neurological disorders, thimerosal currently is at the top of the list of possible culprits being investigated.

Despite official insistence that the evidence linking injected thimerosal to autism is inconclusive, the data suggest otherwise. In 1999 the National Academy of Sciences Institute of Medicine (IOM) must have thought there was something seriously wrong when it supported removal of thimerosal from vaccines, stating that it was "a prudent measure in support of the public goal to reduce mercury exposure of infants and children as much as possible." The IOM further urged that "full consideration be given to removing thimerosal from any biological product to which infants, children and pregnant women are exposed."

A recently published study in the *Journal of American Physicians and Surgeons* by Mark Geier, M.D., Ph.D., and president of the Genetic Centers of America and his son, David Geier, president of Medcon Inc. and a consultant on vaccine cases, was titled "Thimerosal in Childhood Vaccines, Neurodevelopment Disorders and Heart Disease in the United States." It presents strong epidemiological evidence for a link between neurodevelopmental disorders and mercury exposure from thimerosal-containing childhood vaccines.

Specifically, the authors evaluated the doses of mercury that children received as part of their immunization schedule, then compared these doses with federal safety guidelines. Furthermore, to compare the effects of thimerosal in vaccine recipients, the incident rates of neurodevelopmental disorders and heart disease reported to the government's Vaccine Adverse Events Reporting System were analyzed. The results were dramatic. The report revealed that "U.S. infants are exposed to mercury levels from their childhood-immunization schedule that far exceed the EPA [Environmental Protection Agency] and FDA [Food and Drug Administration]–established maximum permissible levels for the daily oral ingestion of methyl mercury."

The authors concluded that "in light of voluminous literature supporting the biologic mechanisms for mercury-induced adverse reactions, the presence of amounts of mercury in thimerosal-containing childhood vaccines exceeding federal safety guidelines for the oral ingestion of mercury and previous epidemiological studies showing adverse reactions to such vaccines, a causal relationship between thimerosal-containing childhood vaccines and neurodevelopment disorders and heart disease appears to be confirmed."

Vaccines May Still Contain Mercury

It is no secret among government and health officials that mercury is toxic and causes serious adverse reactions. In July 1999 the American Academy of Pediatrics and the U.S. Public Health Service issued a joint statement calling for the removal of thimerosal from vaccines. Five years after the joint statement, however, it still is difficult for parents and physicians to be sure that the pharmaceutical companies have indeed removed the toxic substance from their vaccines.

According to Mark Geier, "The 2003 Physicians' Desk Reference [PDR] still shows childhood vaccines containing thimerosal, including diphtheria, tetanus and acellular pertussis. DTaP, manufactured by Aventis Pasteur, contains 25 mcg [25 micrograms] of mercury, Hemophilus influenzae b(Hib) vaccine manufactured by Wyeth contains 25 mcg. of mercury and pediatric Hepatitis B vaccine, manufactured by Merck, contains 12.5 mcg. of mercury."

Mercury and Autism Spectrum Disorders

Seeking answers to her son's [autistic] condition, [Lyn] Redwood turned to the Internet in 1999 and began a search that led to startling discoveries about thimerosal. This vaccine preservative is composed of nearly 50 percent mercury, which is a known neurotoxin especially harmful to fetuses, infants and children. What's more, it has been linked to a range of symptoms collectively known as Autism Spectrum Disorders. At one end is severe autism, in which children are socially withdrawn, do not speak and exhibit bizarre, repetitive, sometimes aggressive behaviors. At the other end are Asperger's Syndrome, a high-functioning form of autism, Pervasive Developmental Disorder (PDD), Attention Deficit Disorder (ADD) and Attention Deficit Hyperactivity Disorder (ADHD).

Annette Fuentes, *In These Times*, December 8, 2003.

Geier continues, "In addition, the influenza vaccine that is recommended for an increasing segment of the pediatric population in the U.S. also contains 25 mcg. of mercury. Assuming that the labeling is correct, it is possible that children in the U.S. in 2003 may be exposed to levels of mercury from thimerosal contained in childhood vaccines that are at higher levels than at any time in the past. Possible total childhood mercury in 2003 is more than 300 mcg. . . ."

Assuming that the package inserts are correct, Geier [states], "The EPA limit is 0.1 micrograms of mercury per kilogram body weight per day. It doesn't take a genius to do the calculations when on their day of birth children are given the hepatitis B vaccine, which is 12.5 micrograms of mercury. The average newborn weighs between 6 and 7 pounds, so they would be allowed 0.3 micrograms of mercury but in this one shot they are getting 12.5 micrograms. That's 39 times more than allowed by law. And it gets worse when you consider that children are getting multiple vaccinations at 2 months. And this limit is for oral ingestion and not injection, which is much worse."

Has Thimerosal Been Removed?

Rhonda Smith, a spokeswoman for the federal Centers for Disease Control and Prevention (CDC), [claims] that, except for mere traces, thimerosal has been removed. "All routinely recommended licensed vaccines," says Smith, "that are currently being manufactured for children in the U.S., except influenza, contain no thimerosal or only trace amounts a concentration of less than 0.0002 percent." But according to the 2003 immunization schedule and the package inserts, there appear to be a number of childhood vaccines that still contain mercury, including those for tetanus and diphtheria. This scenario becomes even more bizarre when one further considers that thimerosal is not a necessary component in vaccines. It first was introduced by pharmaceutical giant Eli Lilly and Co. in the 1930s and is added to vaccines only as a preservative, the theory being that multiple doses are taken from the same bottle and that thimerosal will protect against contamination. However, according to Geier, "the solution to any such problem is to make vaccines available in a single dose, which will cost the pharmaceuticals about one penny more. What is interesting is that if you look up the mumps, measles, rubella [MMR] vaccines in the PDR you'll see that they do not contain thimerosal because it would kill the live virus. The MMR is available in multidose packaging and, yet, there is no preservative. . . . What they did was put a label on it that says 'This product does not contain preservatives. Handle with care.' It's that simple."

Geier insists, "I'm pro-vaccines, but the bottom line is that our kids are getting massive amounts of mercury. Mercury has been withdrawn from everything, including animal vaccines, yet we keep injecting it into our children. Everyone should absolutely refuse to take a vaccine shot that has thimerosal in it, and they should insist on reading the vaccine package insert. Our data showed that the more mercury children received in their childhood vaccines the more neurodevelopment disorders there are. We've looked at this every possible way and every time there's massive evidence to support it."

An Out-of-Control Epidemic

So, if everyone acknowledges the toxicity of mercury and top U.S. health officials have called for its removal, why is thimerosal still in vaccines? "Maybe," concludes Geier, "the mercury isn't being taken out all at once because if the pharmaceutical companies did that you would see an unbelievable change in the rate of autism and there would be massive lawsuits. If you look at the graphs now they go up and up. If you stop the thimerosal all at once you'd see the numbers fall dramatically."

Rep. Dan Burton (R-Ind.), a longtime advocate for victims of autism, has a grandson who became autistic after receiving nine vaccines in one day. Burton recently sent his second request in as many years to the White House asking for a conference of scientists, researchers and parents to look into the causes of autism. The Indiana lawmaker [maintains that] "There is no doubt in my mind that the mercury in vaccines is a major contributing factor to a growing number of neurological disorders among children, but in particular autism."

Burton explains that "thimerosal is a toxic substance mercury and should not be put in close proximity of people, should not be injected into people, especially children who have a newly formed immune system that may not be able to handle it. To my knowledge there never have been long-term tests on thimerosal and we never should have used mercury in vaccines, period. Now what we've got is an epidemic that is absolutely out of control."

The Indiana congressman continues, "One reason this isn't getting the attention it needs is that the Food and Drug Administration has very close ties to the pharmaceutical companies, as does the Department of Health and Human Services [HHS] and the Centers for Disease Control. I've said in the past that in some cases it appears that it's a revolving door and people leave government health agencies and go to work for the pharmaceuticals, which I think have undue influence on our health agencies. Of course, they may not want to look at this because there's a possibility that large claims would be filed and the pharmaceutical companies would have to cough up the money to take care of these kids who have been damaged."

Burton means business. He insists, "The FDA, CDC and HHS should put out in a very public way the dangers of mercury, but as soon as they do it will amount to an admission that their mercury is causing these problems. So the reports that come out of the FDA, CDC and HHS use ambiguous terms. Well, if they're not sure, and there's the remotest possibility that mercury in vaccines could cause autism, they ought to get thimerosal off the market. Too many kids are being ruined for life because of this stuff."

"There is no association between thimerosal-containing vaccines and autism."

Vaccines Do Not Cause Autism

Marie C. McCormick

Marie C. McCormick is a professor at the Harvard School of Public Health and chair of the Institute of Medicine's Committee on Immunization Safety Review. Beginning in 2001, this committee began a comprehensive review of the theories suggesting that vaccines were a cause of autism. In May 2004 the committee released its final report, which concluded that childhood vaccines were not causally related to autism. As McCormick notes in the following viewpoint, there is no evidence that either the MMR (measles/mumps/rubella) vaccines or the vaccines containing mercury preservatives influence the biological mechanisms that are known to have a connection to autism.

As you read, consider the following questions:
1. When did U.S. pharmaceutical companies begin removing thimerosal from vaccines, according to McCormick?
2. According to the author, what were some of the theories on how vaccines might cause autism?
3. In addressing concerns over vaccine safety, what kind of public policy response does the committee recommend, according to McCormick?

The Committee on Immunization Safety Review was established in January 2001 in response to a request from the Centers for Disease Control and Prevention and the National Institutes of Health, both of which recognized the need for an independent group of scientists to address growing concerns about vaccine safety in a timely and objective manner. The committee consists of 13 members with expertise in a variety of relevant public health and medical disciplines.

Since its inception, the committee has issued seven reports. In this eighth and final report, we were asked to revisit concerns about vaccines and autism, specifically whether the vaccine preservative thimerosal or the measles-mumps-rubella— or MMR—vaccine are causally related to autism. The current report follows up two reports examining the role of vaccines in autism that the committee issued in 2001. One reviewed the hypothesized causal association between the MMR vaccine and autism, which the committee rejected based on the evidence at the time. The second report reviewed the hypothesized link between thimerosal-containing vaccines and a broad range of neurodevelopmental disorders including autism. The committee concluded that the evidence available at the time was inadequate to accept or reject a causal relationship between thimerosal and neurodevelopmental disorders.

The report we are releasing today incorporates new epidemiological evidence and studies of biological mechanisms related to vaccines and autism that have emerged since the earlier reports. The committee wishes to emphasize that this report focuses only on autism and does not address other neurodevelopmental disorders.

No Connection Between Vaccines and Autism

Scientists generally agree that most cases of autism likely result from events in the prenatal period or shortly after birth. But there are concerns about the MMR vaccine because autistic symptoms typically do not emerge until the child's second year of life, which is about the same time that the MMR vaccine is first administered. In addition, some point to the apparent increase in the number of reported cases of autism, and question whether this rise may be due, in part, to widespread use of the MMR vaccine and thimerosal-containing vaccines.

The Measles/Mumps/Rubella Vaccine

• MMR vaccine protects children against dangerous, even deadly, diseases.

• Because signs of autism may appear at around the same time children receive the MMR vaccine, some parents may worry that the vaccine causes autism.

• Carefully performed scientific studies have found no relationship between MMR vaccine and autism.

• The CDC continues to recommend two doses of MMR vaccine for all children.

Centers for Disease Control and Prevention, www.cdc.gov, May 2004.

Thimerosal has been used as a preservative to prevent bacterial contamination in multidose vials of several childhood and adult vaccines. The active ingredient in thimerosal is ethylmercury, a close chemical relative of methylmercury. Many forms of mercury are known to damage the nervous system in high doses, although ethylmercury has been studied less than other forms of mercury. In 1999 thimerosal began to be removed from vaccines. This action was taken as a precaution to decrease mercury exposures, despite the absence of data at that time to suggest that thimerosal was in fact dangerous at the levels present in vaccines. As of mid-2000, all childhood vaccines recommended for universal use were available free of thimerosal as a preservative.

On the issue of whether thimerosal is associated with autism, epidemiological studies in the United States, the United Kingdom, Denmark, and Sweden that have been published since our earlier study provided significant evidence that there is no association between thimerosal-containing vaccines and autism. Based on these studies, the committee concluded that the evidence favors rejection of a causal relationship between thimerosal-containing vaccines and autism.

To assess whether the MMR vaccine is associated with autism, the committee looked at the large number of epidemiological studies that have examined this issue. Let me note that the MMR vaccine does not contain and has never contained thimerosal. Fourteen large, well-designed epidemiological studies consistently showed no association between the MMR vaccine and autism. Based on this body of evidence, the committee saw no reason to change its 2001 conclusion that the evidence favors rejection of a causal relationship between the MMR vaccine and autism.

Biological Hypotheses

The committee also reviewed the potential biological mechanisms that have been put forth as possible explanations for how vaccines might cause autism. These hypothesized mechanisms include:

- The release of chemicals into the brain due to disruption of intestinal function by the MMR vaccine.
- Triggering of abnormalities in the immune system that are indicative of damage to the central nervous system induced by vaccines.
- Increased accumulation of mercury and decreased excretion of the element from the brains of a subgroup of children.
- The effects of thimerosal on a variety of biochemical pathways.

The evidence offered for these various hypotheses includes data from in vitro experimental systems, clinical observations, and analogies between rodent behavior and human behavior. While the laboratory observations of the toxic effects of mercury are important in understanding how this metal may cause damage, these observations do not explain how specific exposures in a rapidly developing infant affect certain tissues but not others where these mechanisms are also active. The laboratory studies also have not shown how these effects lead to autism. The committee does not dispute that mercury-containing compounds, including thimerosal, can be very damaging to the nervous system. The question is whether these damaging effects are related to the development of autism.

Autism Is Not Yet Understood

While the committee agreed that the studies raise interesting questions, they do not address the specifics of how these mechanisms result in the symptoms of autism. It is difficult to establish a link between vaccine components and this disorder because scientific understanding about the causes of autism is only in an early stage. Autism is not a single condition but rather a complex set of disorders. It is possible, and perhaps even likely, that autism will be found to have many different causes. It is possible that some people with autism also have abnormal immune reactions, or abnormalities in the way they metabolize mercury. But it is also possible that vaccination does not cause these abnormalities, and likewise that the abnormalities do not lead to autism.

In the absence of experimental or human evidence that either the MMR vaccine or vaccines containing thimerosal affect metabolic, developmental, immune, or other physiological or molecular mechanisms that are causally related to the development of autism, the committee concludes that the hypotheses generated to date are theoretical only.

The committee recommends a public health response that fully supports an array of vaccine safety activities. While the committee strongly supports research that focuses on achieving a better understanding of autism, we recommend that future research be directed toward other lines of inquiry that are supported by current knowledge and evidence, and that offer more promise for finding an answer. Given the current evidence, the vaccine hypothesis doesn't offer that promise.

Improving Communication

The committee also believes that communication with the public about vaccine safety issues needs to be improved. To that end, we recommend developing programs to increase public participation in research on vaccine safety and in policy decisions about the issue. Efforts are also needed to enhance the skills and willingness of scientists and government officials to engage in constructive dialogue with the public about research findings and their policy implications.

"The U.S. military continues to follow a long tradition of using vaccines to protect its members and save lives so that it will be able to fulfill its missions."

Vaccinations Benefit Military Personnel

Ronald D. Harris

Illness and war have a long and complex history, writes Ronald D. Harris in the following viewpoint. Epidemics such as plague, smallpox, and typhoid have often decimated armies, leading to their defeat. For this reason, contends Harris, U.S. military strategy requires the vaccination of troops against all infectious diseases that could be set off by biological weapons. Protecting American troops against dangerous diseases helps ensure that the U.S. military can achieve its goals, he concludes. Harris is a colonel in the U.S. Air Force Reserve.

As you read, consider the following questions:
1. What is variolation, according to the author?
2. What happened when the British Army made the typhoid vaccine optional during the Boer War, according to Harris?
3. As noted by the author, what new vaccines are currently being developed?

Ronald D. Harris, "Why Military Vaccinations Are Important for Force Protection," *The Officer*, vol. 79, June 2003, p. 38. Copyright © 2003 by the Reserve Officers Association of the United States. Reproduced by permission.

History is full of incidents that have altered the course of battle and wars that have hinged upon the administration of medical vaccines to the troops involved. Let me portray several incidents that fall into this realm.

In the Peloponnesian War in 430 B.C., there is historical suggestion that an overwhelming smallpox infection sufficiently reduced the fighting force of the Athenians, so that the Spartans were able to overcome Athenian defenses, resulting in the downfall of Athens.

In A.D. 1346, at the City of Kaffa on the Black Sea, the Tartars catapulted dead bodies of its own plague victims over the walls of the city, which had been under siege. This quickly spread plague throughout the city. The Black Death (plague), which swept through Europe from 1347–1351 and killed more than 25 million (one-third of the population of Europe at that time), was thought to have originated with this event at Kaffa.

Epidemics and War

During the French and Indian War in 1767, Sir Jeffrey Amherst of the British Army ordered a devious plan to defeat Ft. Carillon, which was later named Ft. Ticonderoga. He gave the Indian tribes in the region a "gift" of blankets as a show of friendship. However, the blankets were infected with the smallpox scabs of victims who had previously used the blankets. When the Indians accepted the gifts and brought them back to their villages, they were infected with smallpox, which proceeded to kill almost 80 percent of the tribal members.

In 1776, the Continental Army was engaged in the Battle of Quebec. About 5,500 out of 10,000 American troops, including their commander MG John Thomas, came down with smallpox and died as a result of the disease. The Americans lost this battle and subsequently retreated from Canada. After this extreme lesson on the devastating effect of disease on a fighting force, General Washington in 1777 required all members of the Continental Army to be vaccinated against smallpox, despite a known adverse event incidence of a loss of between 1–2 percent of those variolated (the process of taking material from the scabs or pox pustules and using it to scratch into the skin of a non-infected person to produce a mild form of the disease, thereby reducing the mortality rate of 30 percent down to 1–2 percent and providing lifelong protection against smallpox). The Continental Army never had a problem with smallpox after that. Many American citizens also allowed themselves to be variolated against smallpox because of the devastating effect it was having on the populace.

In 1899 during the Boer War, the British developed the typhoid vaccine. As history has shown, people are usually opposed to vaccines, and the opposition to the typhoid vaccine grew among the British Army troops. Opposition personnel even boarded transport ships in Southampton Harbor and threw the typhoid vaccine into the water. As a result, the British Army made the typhoid vaccine optional and only 14,000 soldiers volunteered to take it. During the Boer War itself, 58,000 British troops contracted typhoid fever and 9,000 needlessly died from the disease. Among those vaccinated, only 2 percent became infected, and they survived. The overall result, however, was that the British lost the Boer War. But a lesson had been learned; in 1914 during World War I, 97 percent of the British troops opted to take the typhoid vaccine.

During World War II, about 99 percent of the American military was vaccinated with smallpox vaccine and there were no cases of smallpox reported among the U.S. forces. Interestingly, there were no reports of any major side effects from the vaccine either and no reports of any deaths among those taking the vaccine. Vaccination against tetanus during World War II led to the fact that only 12 cases of tetanus occurred among American troops, compared with numerous deaths from tetanus among the German Wehrmacht.

A History of Vaccines

Vaccines in general have been around for thousands of years. Around 1000 B.C., the people in India first practiced variolation inoculation. This practice spread to Tibet and eventually made its way to China by monks at a Buddhist monastery in Sichuan province around A.D. 1000. During the 1600s, this process was widely practiced by physicians of the Ottoman Empire.

In 1717, Lady Mary Montagu of London, who had survived smallpox two years earlier, accompanied her husband to Constantinople where he was appointed as the British ambassador. It was there that she learned of the variolation process and insisted that her son be vaccinated against the dreaded smallpox. On return to London in 1721, she persuaded the Prince of Wales to allow a public variolation experiment against smallpox, which was successful. By the 1740s, variolation was popular in England.

The Anthrax Vaccine Is Safe

After examining data from numerous case reports and especially epidemiologic studies, the Committee [to Assess the Safety and Efficacy of the Anthrax Vaccine] concluded that AVA [Anthrax Vaccine Absorbed] is reasonably safe. Within hours or days following vaccination, it is fairly common for recipients to experience some local events (e.g., redness, itching, swelling, or tenderness at the injection site), while a smaller number of vaccine recipients experience some systemic events (e.g., fever and malaise). But these immediate reactions, and the rates at which they occur, are comparable to those observed with other vaccines regularly administered to adults. The committee found no evidence that vaccine recipients face an increased risk of experiencing life-threatening or permanently disabling adverse events immediately after receiving AVA, when compared with the general population. Nor did it find any convincing evidence that vaccine recipients face elevated risk of developing adverse health effects over the longer term, although data are limited in this regard (as they are for all vaccines).

Institute of Medicine, www.iom.edu, March 20, 2002.

In England in 1796, Edward Jenner discovered that a virus similar to another virus could be used to protect people against the deadly smallpox. In 1806, President Thomas Jefferson wrote a letter to Jenner and said: "It is owing to your discovery that in the future peoples of the world will learn about this disgusting smallpox disease only from ancient traditions."

In 1880, William Greenfield in England and then in 1881 Louis Pasteur in Paris discovered a vaccine against the bacteria anthrax. So the road to preventing infectious diseases was being paved with scientific discovery about the mechanism of disease production and the ways to short-circuit their destructive ways. In spite of these advances, smallpox continued to spread rapidly throughout the world up through the 20th century and resulted in almost 500 million deaths in the 20th century alone. As late as 1966, there were 2 million deaths from smallpox in that year alone. Not until the Global Eradication Program, sponsored by the World Health Organization, was fully put into effect was smallpox successfully eradicated in 1980 as a naturally occurring disease and smallpox vaccinations stopped being necessary worldwide.

Protecting Troops

The United States has had an active defensive biological weapons program that dates back to 1969 when President [Richard] Nixon declared that the United States would not develop any offensive biological weapons but would concentrate only on developing defensive measures against biological agents. It has become part of the overall U.S. military strategy to protect our military forces against all naturally occurring infectious diseases, as well as those potential diseases that could be inflicted on a battlefield by the use of biological weapons agents. As a result, U.S. forces receive vaccination protection against yellow fever, typhoid, hepatitis A and B, as well as others necessary, depending on the particular theater to which troops are sent. Because of the known threat of biological weapons from adversaries such as Iraq, and based upon knowledge of prior Soviet bioweapons programs, the decision was made to vaccinate U.S. troops against anthrax and, more recently, smallpox.

Vaccines that protect against numerous other agents are currently undergoing research protocols. Among those are research on vaccines for botulinum, Q-fever, plague, tularemia, and hemorrhagic fever viruses such as Ebola, Marburg and Rift Valley Fever. New vaccines for anthrax and smallpox are also being developed.

Although there are and always have been groups of citizens throughout history who have opposed vaccines and their use, it is estimated that of the four major contributions of medicine to the longevity of people (proper hygiene, clean water, antibiotics and vaccines), vaccines are credited with saving more lives than the others except for the advent of clean water. It is and has been Department of Defense [DoD] policy to use only FDA [Food and Drug Administration]-licensed and approved vaccines for its troops. Starting back in 1997, there was considerable controversy relating to the use of the anthrax vaccine. It will be comforting to all that a thorough review of the anthrax program was carried out by the American National Academy of Sciences' Institute of Medicine (IOM). In its report, published in March 2002, IOM stated that the DoD anthrax vaccine immunization program was a safe and effective program to prevent anthrax of all types. Therefore, the U.S. military continues to follow a long tradition of using vaccines to protect its members and save lives so that it will be able to fulfill its missions. The current military smallpox vaccination program is being coordinated with the CDC [Centers for Disease Control] and uses only FDA-licensed vaccines to protect DoD forces. DoD provides numerous other mechanisms to protect its troops, including protective clothing and breathing apparatus and the use of appropriate antibiotics, but the only around-the-clock continual protection against biological agents is vaccinations.

So, as you see, diseases and vaccines have had a profound impact on the outcomes of warfare throughout history. We are fortunate to live in a time when we can rely on our medical resources to help prevent diseases, and we are also fortunate to live in a country that provides this protection for its people.

"There have been a rash of unexplained deaths and illnesses among both deployed and non-deployed soldiers following vaccination."

Vaccinations Have Harmed Military Personnel

John Richardson

The U.S. armed forces have been administering unapproved and unsafe vaccines to American service members, contends John Richardson in the following viewpoint. A rash of illnesses, such as pneumonia, multiple sclerosis, and auto-immune disorders—as well as several deaths—have been linked with the anthrax and smallpox vaccines given to all troops sent to Iraq in 2003, writes Richardson. These cases remain largely unexamined and ignored, he points out, and are part of a recurring pattern of Defense Department neglect and denial of medical problems in the military. Richardson was a fighter pilot during the 1991 Gulf War, and he later served as a policy analyst for the Joint Chiefs of Staff and as a military fellow at Harvard University. He is currently a consultant to the National Gulf War Resource Center, a veteran's organization.

As you read, consider the following questions:
1. What happened to Army Specialist Rachel Lacy, according to the author?
2. In Richardson's opinion, what strategy does the Pentagon tend to adopt when confronting medical problems in the military?

On January 14, 2002, two fellow military officers and I met with the Pentagon's newly-appointed top doctor, William Winkenwerder, M.D., to brief him on the military's anthrax vaccination program criticized in 11 prior General Accounting Office reports. I told Dr. Winkenwerder, a civilian, that he held a key Constitutional responsibility—the "civilian control" of military medicine—and that he needed to address deep systemic problems, starting with the vaccination program.

But Dr. Winkenwerder—a career hospital administrator—ignored our concerns and yielded to his military staff. Over the next year he authorized the resumption of mandatory anthrax and smallpox vaccinations. While the British and Australian military made the shots voluntary during the Iraq War, American servicemembers who refused vaccination were—and still are—being court-martialed and jailed. In contrast, the highest judge in the Canadian military ruled in 2000 that the mandatory use of the U.S. anthrax vaccine was a violation of the Canadian Charter of Human Rights. Apparently, American soldiers have no such rights.

The Death of Rachel Lacy

The more serious consequences of Dr. Winkenwerder's decision are now becoming clear. On Tuesday, Dec. 2 [2003], he belatedly announced that the death of Army Specialist Rachel Lacy [in] April [2003] was "probably" caused by vaccines, among them the controversial anthrax and smallpox shots given to all soldiers sent to Iraq.

This admission follows a familiar pattern we've seen with Gulf War illness in the 1991 Persian Gulf War, with Agent Orange in Vietnam War and with other military medical problems. First, the Pentagon denies responsibility. Then, they claim the death or illness is unique. And finally, they blame the victim.

Equally important, this case highlights the bipartisan indifference of a Congress that for decades has refused to hold the military accountable for law-breaking and unethical behavior related to its practice of medicine. The Pentagon has a well-established pattern of ignoring laws passed by Congress intended to protect soldiers' health. For instance, the

Pentagon refused to create baseline medical records of all deployed Iraq War troops, as required under a 1997 law. And with the anthrax vaccine used on Rachel Lacy, the Pentagon ignored a 1998 law barring the military from using drugs and vaccines unapproved for their intended use without a presidential executive order.

"A Rare and Tragic Case"?

Rachel Lacy's story is simple. She received five shots in one day and later became ill and died. In her case, the Army's admission comes after seven months of denials that vaccines caused her death. Dr. Winkenwerder asserts that her death is a "rare and tragic case," but investigations by United Press International and CBS News suggest that there have been a rash of unexplained deaths and illnesses among both deployed and non-deployed soldiers following vaccination.

For instance, the Army has attempted to attribute pneumonia deaths overseas to Iraqi cigarettes and dust, when virtually identical cases have occurred in domestically based soldiers who were vaccinated. The Army ignores the possibility that these deaths were caused by vaccines, despite Navy doctors having linked anthrax vaccine to a pneumonia-like autoimmune disorder called hypersensitivity pneumonitis.

Additionally, news reports of soldiers at Ft. Stewart, Ga., and Ft. Knox, Ky. being kept in "medical hold" units without adequate medical care have revealed few of the sick soldiers had combat-related illnesses—and most had not even deployed. Their illnesses included multiple sclerosis and other autoimmune disorders that the Army refuses to investigate. Like Lacy, the Army has blamed many of these sick reservist soldiers—who were healthy enough to be ordered to combat—for having preexisting conditions that caused their illnesses.

Finally, while acknowledging that vaccines played a role in Lacy's death, the Pentagon is once again engaging in a 'blame-the-victim' strategy, by ascribing her death to a predisposition to Lupus. This was discovered by evaluating a 1998 sample of SPC Lacy's blood the Army already had in its possession—which raises the question of why the Army doesn't screen soldiers in advance instead of waiting until they become ill or die from vaccine-related complications.

The answer, sadly, is that common sense doesn't have a place in military medicine when it conflicts with perceived operational necessity or inflexible doctrinal precepts.

Systemic Medical Abuse

Recent reports in the *New England Journal of Medicine* found that genetic differences contribute to development of autoimmune disorders and that these diseases may take years to develop. These findings call into question the military's rigidly uniform vaccination policies, and contradict the Pentagon's frequent assertions that post-vaccination autoimmune illnesses that develop weeks or months afterwards are not caused by the shots.

Yet, the military has stated Lacy's death will not cause a change in their immunization policies—including multiple, near-simultaneous injections. The time has come for Congress to stop the Department of Defense's continued medical abuse of America's military service members. Instead, most members passively allow wrongdoing—known to the Pentagon leadership and to Congress—to go unpunished.

A Serious Human Rights Concern

Vaccination of armed services personnel raises a serious human rights concern. Although vaccination of health workers and the general public involves voluntary, individual decisions (at least as of this writing), smallpox vaccination of armed services personnel is mandatory absent a medical exemption. Those who do not qualify for medical exemptions may be disciplined if they refuse vaccination. Such punishment can be serious: service members who refused anthrax vaccination during the 1990s were sometimes court-martialed or discharged. The problem posed by mandatory vaccination is basic: military service does not negate humanity and basic human rights.

Thomas May, *Human Rights*, Spring 2003.

For instance, in early 2000, 73 officers filed a complaint with the DoD [Department of Defense] Inspector General over false and misleading statements made to Congress on anthrax vaccine safety by the top general in the Air National

Guard. After twice refusing to investigate, the DoD Inspector General cited the general for violations of the DoD Joint Ethics Regulation. But the Pentagon leadership and Congress allowed this general to remain on active duty.

More recently, the DoD Inspector General has failed to refer for prosecution three now-retired senior officers who misled Congress and military courts about anthrax vaccine safety. Two of these officers later received payments from the anthrax vaccine manufacturer, BioPort Corporation, after they retired. While the DoD Inspector General deemed these payments ethical, the allegations about giving false testimony have been referred to the FBI Public Corruption Unit. But there is little reason to expect the FBI to investigate, given that the Department of Justice is currently defending the legality of Pentagon's anthrax vaccine program in federal court.

The Need for Congressional Response

Unfortunately, the relevant Armed Services and Veterans Affairs committees have been swayed that anthrax and smallpox vaccines are necessary by unproven assertions of a bioterror threat. So, oversight of military medicine has been left to a handful of courageous Congressmen, such as Rep. Christopher Shays, R-Conn., and Sen. Jeff Bingaman, D-N.M., who, unfortunately, lack the jurisdiction—and support from colleagues—to force the military to obey the law and conform to accepted ethical standards in their practice of medicine.

The illnesses and deaths of soldiers from the medical friendly fire should have already prompted Congress to intervene and redirect the Pentagon's troop health protection programs. Sadly, such aggressive congressional oversight of military medicine is still needed.

The first step toward Pentagon accountability should be a bipartisan call for the resignation of Dr. Winkenwerder and an independent criminal investigation of the medical corps officers responsible for the DoD anthrax and smallpox vaccination programs. If the unnecessary deaths of soldiers doesn't demand a congressional response, what does?

Periodical Bibliography

The following articles have been selected to supplement the diverse views presented in this chapter.

Douglas S. Barasch   "How Safe Are Kids' Vaccines?" *Good Housekeeping*, September 2000.

Ceci Connolly   "The Vaccination Preoccupation," *Washington Post National Weekly Edition*, March 17–23, 2003.

Madeline Drexler   "A Pox on America," *Nation*, April 28, 2003.

Victoria Stagg Elliott   "Polio Nearly Gone; Should Vaccine End Too?" *American Medical News*, January 14, 2002.

Annette Fuentes   "Autism in a Needle? The Toxic Tale of Vaccinations and Mercury Poisoning," *In These Times*, December 8, 2003.

Carolyn Gard   "How Vaccines Work: A Little Pain in the Arm Now Eliminates a Lot of Pain Later," *Current Health*, November 2001.

Peter J. Hotez   "Vaccine Diplomacy," *Foreign Policy*, May 2001.

Aimee Howd   "When Vaccines Do Harm to Kids," *Insight on the News*, February 28, 2000.

Sally Koch Kubetin   "Vaccine, Autism Link Not Supported by the Data: Institute of Medicine Hearing," *Family Practice News*, March 15, 2004.

Rich Lowry   "The Democrats' War on Vaccines," *Conservative Chronicle*, December 16, 2002.

Thomas May   "Armed Services Smallpox Vaccination: Medical Research and Military Necessity," *Human Rights*, Spring 2003.

Wendy Orent   "Vaccines as a First Line of Defense," *Los Angeles Times*, October 20, 2002.

Edmund Sanders   "U.S. Weighs Risk of Smallpox, and Risk of Smallpox Vaccine," *Los Angeles Times*, June 16, 2002.

Miriam E. Tucker   "Multiple Vaccines Not Tied to Immune Dysfunction," *Pediatric News*, February 2002.

Sarah Wildman   "The Real Biothreat: Drop Shot," *New Republic*, June 17, 2002.

John A.T. Young and R. John Collier   "Attacking Anthrax," *Scientific American*, March 2002.

CHAPTER 4

How Can Food-Borne Illness Be Prevented?

Chapter Preface

At the beginning of the twenty-first century, scientists and medical experts were disturbed by reports that a considerable increase in the rate of food-borne illness had occurred in the United States between 1994 and 1999. The rate of illnesses caused by food had increased by as much as tenfold in just a few years, according to Physicians and Scientists for Responsible Application of Science and Technology. Further investigations led to disquieting theories about the reasons for the upsurge in food-borne illness. Sweden, for example, had experienced no increase in food-borne infections between 1994 and 1999. Moreover, notes food biotechnology expert Mae-Wan Ho, the United States and Sweden experienced profoundly different rates of virally based illness during those years. In Sweden, viruses were the cause of only 9 percent of illnesses during the mid- and late 1990s; in the United States, viruses were the cause of 80 percent of illnesses. According to Ho, the use of genetically engineered (GE) foods has increased greatly in the United States since 1994. Sweden, however, consumed almost no GE foods between 1994 and 1999. Ho suspects that GE foods might be triggering the emergence of new human viruses.

Genetic engineering enables scientists to create plants, animals, and microorganisms by manipulating genes in a way that does not occur naturally. This controversial technology has been applied to fruits and vegetables to improve crop yields, boost specific nutrients, enhance flavors, hinder insects and other pests, and to create other useful modifications to food for human consumption. However, as Ho and other concerned scientists point out, GE food plants contain components of virus genes that are similar to human virus genes, increasing the chances of unanticipated DNA combinations and genetic mutations that can create new viruses. Moreover, there are toxins and bacterial DNA sequences in almost all GE foods that increase the chances of intestinal irritation, which in turn may cause acute or long-term gastrointestinal illnesses.

But many genetic experts discount the suggestions of Ho and other GE food critics. According to Patrick Bateson, the biological secretary of the Royal Society of the United Kingdom, there is no evidence that food from genetically modified plants causes food-borne illness in humans. What has happened, he maintains, is that theories about the negative consequences of genetic engineering have been restated as fact. As Bateson argues, "The public have been told for several years that genetically modified foods are inherently unsafe to eat. Most people would like to know what evidence exists to back up such claims. We have examined the results of published research, and have found nothing to indicate that [GE] foods are inherently unsafe. If anybody does have convincing evidence, get it out in the open so that it can be evaluated." Moreover, as many experts point out, GE foods may actually create new protections against illness. Charles Arntzen of Arizona State University, for example, has been combining his knowledge of molecular genetics with earlier studies of vaccines in hopes of altering plant DNA to produce food that can prevent deadly diseases.

The question of whether modern food production technologies help to create or prevent illness will remain a subject of heated debate in the coming years. The authors in the following chapter present differing opinions on food processing and sanitation techniques and their effects on human health.

| "*The failure of state and federal agencies to take swift action [concerning the threat of mad cow disease] is inexcusable.*"

The Government Should Act Quickly to Protect the Public from Mad Cow Disease

Joel Bleifuss

"Mad cow disease," or bovine spongiform encephalopathy (BSE), was first discovered in Britain among cattle that had been fed supplements containing parts of sheep infected with scrapie, a degenerative neurological disease. In the 1990s the British government announced that some people had contracted a human form of BSE after consuming the meat of cattle with the disease. Britain destroyed its infected herds and changed its beef production policies as a result. In the following viewpoint Joel Bleifuss argues that the U.S. government has been negligent in protecting consumers from the dangers of mad cow disease. Federal agencies charged with guarding public health deny that the disease is a threat to consumers and appear to be more concerned with protecting the U.S. beef industry, states Bleifuss. Bleifuss is the editor of *In These Times*, a biweekly news journal.

As you read, consider the following questions:

1. What are the various forms of the human strain of transmissible spongiform encephalopathy, according to Bleifuss?
2. What is chronic wasting disease, according to the author?

Joel Bleifuss, "The First Stone," *In These Times*, vol. 28, February 16, 2004, pp. 12–13. Copyright © 2004 by *In These Times*, www.inthesetimes.com. Reproduced by permission.

The unfolding story of mad cow disease follows an all-too-familiar and damning pattern. A threat to public health is discovered, the affected industries and their allies in government respond with a public relations campaign, the evidence mounts and some reforms are implemented. This is followed by more evidence and more reforms. Yet nowhere in this scenario have the federal agencies charged with protecting public health—the Food and Drug Administration (FDA), the U.S. Department of Agriculture (USDA), and the Centers for Disease Control and Prevention—taken proactive steps to remedy the situation. Rather, they have operated in the interests of huge agriculture and food lobbies.

Since 1993, I have devoted numerous [columns] to mad cow and related diseases. Nearly every prediction—and warning—from scientists who are experts in this field has come to pass. Yet, by and large, the mainstream media have chosen to listen to the palliative pronouncements of government officials and industry flacks. With mad cow disease now established in the United States that may be changing.

How Now Mad Cow

Mad cow, first discovered in Great Britain in 1985, is a type of malady known as transmissible spongiform encephalopathy (TSE). The disease gets its name from the sponge-like formations that occur in the brains of infected mammals. The sheep form of the disease, which has been recognized since 1755, is known as scrapie. In Britain, cattle contracted mad cow disease, known as Bovine Spongiform Encephalopathy (BSE), by eating protein feed supplements that contained scrapie-infected sheep.

The human strain of TSE comes in several forms, including Creutzfeldt-Jacob disease (CJD), Kuru (a TSE that several decades ago plagued a population of New Guinea cannibals before changes in dietary laws), and new variant CJD (nvCJD), the form of the disease that comes from eating infected cattle.

The USDA has long known that mad cow disease posed a threat. However, department officials were worried about danger to the industry—not the public. In 1991, the USDA prepared contingency plans to deal with the possibility that mad cow disease could rear its ugly head in the United States. To wit, it drew up a strategy paper titled "BSE Public Relations." That plan reads in part, "The mere perception that BSE might exist in the United States could have devastating effects on our domestic markets for beef and dairy." And it noted that the agricultural industry is "vulnerable to media scrutiny" regarding "the practice of feeding rendered ruminant products to ruminants and the risk to human health" that might stem from this practice.

Mad Cows in America

To all indications, and contrary to recent news reports, an American strain of BSE has long been circulating through the food chain. In 1985, a Stentsonville, Wisconsin, mink ranch was wiped out by transmissible mink encephalopathy. The diet of the mink consisted of 5 percent horsemeat and 95 percent "downer cows"—cows so lame they fall down and are unable to get up.

Could one of those downer cows fed to the mink have been infected with an American strain of BSE? In December 1992, the late Richard Marsh, a veterinary scientist at the University of Wisconsin, reported on experiments in Mission, Texas, and Ames, Iowa, where brain matter from scrapie-infected American sheep was injected into the brains of cows. The infected cows developed BSE, but their symptoms differed from the mad cow disease that was plaguing Europe. In May 1993, Marsh told me, "The signs that these cattle showed were not the widely recognized signs of BSE—not signs of mad cow disease. What they showed was what you might expect from a downer cow." In other words, BSE-infected cattle in Europe went mad before dying, but BSE-infected cows in the United States simply fell down and died. Each year in the United States about 150,000 cattle suffer from downer cow syndrome. Those downer cows that made it out of the pasture alive ended up in the slaughterhouse and into the food chain. Until 1996, when the practice was banned by the USDA, the slaughterhouse remains of at least 14 percent of all cattle, including downer cows, were rendered into protein and fed back to other cows as feed supplements. What's more, the meat from these tough and old downer cows usually ended up in fast-food hamburgers and other highly processed meat products—that is until the slaughter of downer cows was halted by Agriculture Secretary Ann Veneman on December 30, 2003.

"The USDA tends to respond to commodity groups rather than the consumer. And the government hasn't taken any measures to restrict what goes into animal feed," Marsh said in 1993. "The Center for Veterinary Medicine at the FDA would have to make the recommendation not to feed ruminant animals to cattle, but we can't get them to do this."

Breaking News in Britain

In 1996, the USDA belatedly decided it was time to stop feeding the rendered protein from ruminants (cows, sheep and deer) to other ruminants. The department had considered implementing such policies in 1991 but decided not to because such regulations "could pose major problems for the U.S. livestock, feed and rendering industry," according to "BSE Rendering Policies," an internal 1991 USDA report.

The impetus for this ban was the breaking news in Britain that some people, mostly young, were beginning to die agonizing deaths from a new kind of CJD (nvCJD), the cause of which, as the British government acknowledged, was consumption of mad cow meat. The British Ministry of Health discovered this new form of the disease because it had set up a registry for CJD.

However in the United States, the USDA, in its "BSE Public Relations" plan, advised the department to "avoid the public relations problems such as have occurred in the U.K," such as setting up a registry of CJD cases that "appeared to legitimize concern about a link between BSE and human health."

Variable Symptoms

In the last three years, studies have suggested that classical CJD might be caused by eating BSE-infected cattle, according to a recent report by Todd Hartman in the *Rocky Mountain News*.

In Great Britain, scientists injected BSE into mice whose brains were genetically engineered with human genes. While some of the mice developed nvCJD, the kind people get from eating mad cows, other mice came down with classical CJD. In their November 2002 report, the scientists wrote, "This finding has important potential implications as it raises the possibility that some humans infected with [mad cow disease] may develop clinical diseases indistinguishable from classical CJD." And in 2003, French scientists discovered that scrapie, the sheep TSE, caused brain damage in mice similar to that of classical CJD.

Kal. © 2004 by the *Baltimore Sun*. Reproduced by permission.

Hartman writes, "The two studies suggest that at least some of the hundreds of Americans who contract classical CJD each year could have been infected by BSE-contaminated meat, and not simply by biological bad luck."

How common CJD in its various forms is in the United States is unclear. Some medical experts believe that the incidence of CJD in the U.S. population is much higher than the commonly assumed 1 per million. A 1989 study at the University of Pittsburgh examined the case histories of 54 demented patients who, upon their death, were autopsied at the University of Pittsburgh. The study discovered that 39 (72 percent) of the patients had Alzheimer's; 15 (27.7 percent) had central nervous system disorders; and three (5.5 percent) had CJD. The researchers concluded that the three cases of CJD turned up in their study "had a much longer course than is usually seen with that condition and failed [when the patient was alive] to show the usual EEG abnormalities." In other words, the CJD cases discovered in Pittsburgh exhibited symptoms that were more compatible with Alzheimer's disease than classical CJD.

A 1989 Yale University study reported similar findings. Postmortem examination of 46 patients diagnosed with Alzheimer's revealed that six (13 percent) actually had CJD.

An Unrecognized Form of the Illness?

The Pittsburgh and Yale studies point to the possibility that some of the 4 million people in the United States suffering from Alzheimer's may actually be infected with the agent that causes CJD. And that raises this question: Has an unrecognized form of BSE infected U.S. cattle and entered the human food chain?

Bolstering this concern is a report from the *Philadelphia Inquirer* that seven people in New Jersey have died from classical CJD, all of whom ate at the same racetrack in Cherry Hill, New Jersey.

The scope of CJD incidence in humans is further complicated by the fact that a deer form of mad cow disease, known as chronic wasting disease, is endemic in parts of Wyoming, Colorado and Wisconsin. At least two young hunters who ate and dressed deer have come down with CJD. And a third, a young woman who ate venison from a deer shot in Maine, also contracted the disease. Because CJD is overwhelmingly a disease of the old, the young age of the current victims raises the strong possibility that they contracted the disease through eating deer suffering from chronic wasting disease.

In 1999, Paul Brown, an expert on TSE at the National Institutes of Health, told John Stauber, author of *Mad Cow U.S.A.*, that deer hunters must be out of their minds to be consuming deer in areas where chronic wasting disease is prevalent. That health warning, however, has not been given to the general public. "The failure of state and federal agencies to take swift action and warn hunters about potential risks of chronic wasting disease is inexcusable," Stauber said at the time.

Why the silence? One reason could be that state wildlife departments are heavily dependent on income derived from licenses for big game. The Colorado Wildlife Division maintains that chronic wasting disease does not affect humans. Yet at the same time it advises hunters to "wear rubber gloves when field dressing carcasses, minimize handling of brain and spinal column and wash hands afterwards"—and then go home and feast on venison, though not the "brain, spinal cord, eyes, spleen and lymph nodes of harvested animals."

| *"The notion that people can contract a human form of [mad cow] disease by eating beef from infected cows is more bun than burger."*

Mad Cow Disease Is Not a Serious Threat to the Public

Steven Milloy

The dangers of mad cow disease for humans have been greatly exaggerated, contends Steven Milloy in the following viewpoint. Although mad cow disease is similar to a rare human neurological disorder known as new variant Creutzfeldt-Jakob disease (nvCJD), the allegation that nvCJD is caused by the consumption of beef infected with mad cow disease is unproven, Milloy reports. While cattle infected with mad cow disease should be destroyed to prevent an epidemic among the animals, there is no evidence showing that eating cooked meat from infected cattle is dangerous to humans. Milloy is the publisher of JunkScience.com and an adjunct scholar at the Cato Institute, a libertarian think tank based in Washington, D.C.

As you read, consider the following questions:
1. When and where did the first epidemic of mad cow disease occur, according to Milloy?
2. According to the author, what caused researchers to suspect that mad cow disease might be connected to new variant Creutzfeldt-Jakob disease?
3. What is kuru, according to Milloy?

Mad cow disease was diagnosed in a Canadian cow [in May 2003] setting off a new round of predictable but groundless panic.[1]

The U.S. government promptly banned imports of Canadian beef and cattle. Investors dumped the stock of beef-related companies, notably McDonald's, which lost US$1.5-billion in market value.

And, of course, what health scare would be complete without media hype?

Front-page coverage in the *New York Times*, for example, reported that eating meat from diseased cattle has allegedly caused more than 100 human deaths in Europe since 1994 and "raised questions about the health benefits of eating beef for many consumers around the world."

There's no question that bovine spongiform encephalopathy (BSE), commonly called "mad cow," is a highly infectious, neurological disease in cattle. But the notion that people can contract a human form of the disease by eating beef from infected cows is more bun than burger.

A New Brain Disease

The first epidemic of mad cow broke out among cattle in the United Kingdom in 1986. Beginning in 1994, human cases of a supposedly novel brain disease, called new variant Creutzfeldt-Jakob disease (nvCJD), began appearing in the U.K.

Though laboratory testing seemed to indicate BSE and nvCJD were similar, no one could determine with certainty whether and how BSE was related to nvCJD. There were no geographic areas in the U.K. with a significantly higher incidence of people with nvCJD and there were no cases of nvCJD among "high-risk" groups such as farmers, slaughterhouse workers or butchers.

When researchers considered the possibility that nvCJD was caused by consumption of beef from BSE-infected cattle, no correlations could be established between nvCJD and any specific meat or dairy product because consumption was so widespread. Moreover, no one could establish whether any of

1. In December 2003 a cow in Washington State was diagnosed with mad cow disease.

the nvCJD cases ever consumed beef from diseased cattle.

Researchers nevertheless became fixated on the idea consumption of infected beef was the culprit behind nvCJD after it was discovered that 1980s slaughterhouse practices and meat preparation inadvertently might have allowed diseased tissue to be mixed into a variety of packaged meat products such as hot dogs, sausages, beef patties and luncheon meats.

Mad cow mania was on.

Flaws of the Infected Beef Theory

But the infected beef theory doesn't explain why nvCJD tended to occur in young people—most cases have occurred among 15- to 25-year olds. It doesn't offer the slightest clue as to why only about 130 nvCJD cases have occurred in a British population of 60 million exposed to potentially contaminated beef products.

Some have suggested that a kind of "epidemiological Russian roulette" is at work, where consumption of infected beef results in rare and randomly distributed cases of nvCJD. The Russian roulette explanation is not a scientific one, however, and not one on which public alarm or public policy should be based.

Despite its gaping holes, the infected beef theory has mutated into orthodoxy among many in the medical and public health community that few have been brave enough to challenge.

A Nonexistent Epidemic

One U.K. public health expert, George A. Venters, did manage to have an article published in the *British Medical Journal* in October, 2001, titled, "New variant Creutzfeld-Jakob disease: the epidemic that never was."

Venters maintains the infected beef theory is wrong and that nvCJD might not even be a new disease. He challenged the biological plausibility of BSE causing nvCJD, since no direct evidence exists that the vehicle of BSE infection—a special protein called a prion—is infectious to humans. Nor is there direct evidence that BSE prions survive cooking, digestion and the human immune system.

Venters points out that the clinical features and pathology of nvCJD are similar to kuru, a prion disease found in Papua New Guinea and spread by cannibalism. The differences in pathology between kuru and nvCJD, Venters says, may be more of degree than kind since nvCJD patients tend to live longer because they get better medical care.

If nvCJD is not a novel disease, it can't be tied back to BSE-infected meat from the 1986 mad cow epidemic.

After discussing the numerous deficiencies in the BSE-nvCJD hypothesis, Venters observed, "The evidence that has been amassed is directed toward confirming the [BSE-nvCJD] hypothesis rather than testing it. Salient contrary information has either been played down or ignored."

BSE-infected cattle should be isolated and destroyed to ensure there is no further spread of mad cow disease among the animals. There is no dispute about that. But nvCJD is a rare and apparently random disease of uncertain origin. There is no justification for even the slightest concern about the safety of Canadian beef.

"Scientists are providing us with valuable ways to enhance the safety of our world's food supplies."

New Technologies Can Help Prevent Food-Borne Illness

B.G. Scott

Cutting-edge technologies are helping to reduce the incidence of food-borne illness, contends B.G. Scott in the following viewpoint. Applying knowledge drawn from the life sciences, physics, and engineering, scientists are significantly enhancing the sensitivity and efficiency of methods to protect food supplies from harmful microbes and chemicals. Genetic engineering, biotechnology, and food irradiation are useful for either detecting or destroying food-borne pathogens, the author explains. Scott is a New Jersey–based freelance writer who specializes in science and technology issues.

As you read, consider the following questions:
1. According to Scott, how many U.S. residents are hospitalized each year because of food-borne illness?
2. How is a diode array spectrophotometer used to detect food contamination, according to the author?
3. According to Scott, what are "sentinel plants" and how might they be used to detect harmful microbes and chemicals?

B.G. Scott, "Keeping Our Food Safe," *World & I*, vol. 18, September 2003, pp. 136–43. Copyright © 2003 by News World Communications, Inc. Reproduced by permission.

Does this milk taste sour? Does that uncooked hamburger meat look brown and smell bad? Is that a gray fuzz growing on those strawberries? Do you see a blue mold on the bread? When we select food from the grocery store or get something to eat at home, we normally inspect it in various ways to ensure that it is still healthy to eat. If it looks, smells, or tastes bad, we know we need to avoid it.

Too often, though, our senses cannot detect spoiled or contaminated food. We may find out only after eating it and becoming ill. In most cases, the illness is minor, such as a brief spell of diarrhea, vomiting, or nausea. In some cases, however, food poisoning is more serious and may even be fatal if not treated immediately.

Addressing Food Contamination

By now, scientists have identified a long list of organisms and substances that can contaminate food. They include dozens of pathogenic (disease-causing) bacteria, such as *Campylobacter*, *Salmonella*, *Staphylococcus*, *Escherichia coli* O157:H7, and *Clostridium*. In addition, there are foodborne viruses—such as the rotaviruses—that make us sick, and various molds, including *Aspergillus* species, that produce poisons called *mycotoxins*. Moreover, there are scores of chemical contaminants, including pesticides, metals, and toxic residues from food processing or drug manufacturing.

To prevent food contamination, public health experts teach food handlers and consumers basic principles about food safety, such as the importance of maintaining hygienic conditions, washing raw produce, storing food at cold temperatures, and cooking it at sufficiently high temperatures to kill dangerous microbes. In addition, in most nations of the developed world, businesses that store, handle, and sell food have to follow strict regulations.

In the United States, the Food and Drug Administration (FDA) enforces such regulations and inspects food production lines. Other agencies, particularly at the state and local levels, inspect stores, restaurants, and even street vendors' carts to ensure that the food being sold is safe for consumption. As a result, America's food supplies are among the safest in the world.

179

Yet, food contamination continues to be a problem, even in this country. The Centers for Disease Control and Prevention (CDC) estimates that roughly one-fourth of all U.S. residents suffer from foodborne illnesses each year (although 98 percent of cases go unreported), leading to 325,000 hospitalizations and 5,000 deaths. The annual cost associated with these illnesses has been estimated to exceed $7.7 billion. Moreover, the threat of terrorist attacks raises the possibility of deliberate contamination of food supplies and further exacerbation of the problem.

A New Generation of Technologies

To tackle this problem, scientists at universities and research centers across the United States are designing a new generation of sophisticated technologies based on knowledge combined from various disciplines, particularly microbiology, chemistry, physics, and engineering. The new instruments will provide higher efficiency and sensitivity for the detection or removal of microbial and chemical contaminants of food supplies.

For example, several laboratories of the Agricultural Research Service (ARS) have been designing automated devices to inspect large quantities of food at high speeds. One system, involving an instrument called a *diode array spectrophotometer*, was developed by a research team led by agricultural engineer Yud-Ren Chen, at the ARS Instrumentation and Sensing Laboratory in Beltsville, Maryland. It can check chicken carcasses for wholesomeness at a rate of up to 180 birds per minute.

Each defeathered bird is illuminated with a spot of light (about 1 inch in diameter) from a tungsten-halogen lamp. The light has a spectrum of wavelengths—from the visible range of colors to the invisible, near-infrared region—and different parts of the spectrum are reflected at different intensities from the chicken skin. The reflected light is picked up by the spectrophotometer, sent to a computer, and analyzed by special software to identify defects and possible systemic diseases. A bird with a possible problem can be quickly removed from the production line.

A second system designed and tested by the Beltsville lab

is based on a concept called *multispectral imaging*. In this case, the entire chicken carcass is illuminated with light from a tungsten-halogen lamp, and a "common-aperture" camera (equipped with special filters and sensors) takes three digital images of each bird at three different wavelengths of reflected light. These images are transmitted to a computer, which analyzes them to check for wholesomeness and localized problems such as tumors. The rate of inspection is about 90 birds per minute. This system has recently been adapted to check apples for bruises and contamination with fecal matter. It may eventually be extended to inspect fruits and vegetables in general.

A similar multispectral imaging system, designed and patented by the ARS Poultry Processing and Meat Quality Research Unit in Athens, Georgia, inspects chickens for contaminants such as fecal matter and partially digested food from ruptured chicken crops. This apparatus is capable of operating at 180 birds per minute. A third system, now commercially available, was developed at the Preharvest Food Safety and Enteric Disease Research Unit in Ames, Iowa. It uses fluorescent imaging to look for fecal contamination on cattle carcasses.

Fluorescent Plants and Bacteria

At Pennsylvania State University (Penn State), molecular biologist Ramesh Raina and chemical ecologist Jack Schultz are collaborating on experiments to produce "sentinel" plants—that is, genetically engineered plants that glow when exposed to harmful microbes or chemicals in the environment. It may sound far-fetched, but they have taken a jellyfish gene (named *gfp*, for *green fluorescent protein*) and inserted it into the DNA of a small flowering plant known as *Arabidopsis*. The jellyfish gene is attached to an "on-off" switch (called a *promoter*) in the plant DNA.

When the plant senses a particular microbe or chemical in its environment, it sends a biochemical signal from the surface of its cells to the DNA. If this signal switches the promoter on, the *gfp* gene is activated and starts producing green fluorescent protein. As a result, the plant emits a green glow when illuminated by ultraviolet (UV) light.

Raina and Schultz plan to engineer a whole array of plants with inserted *gfp* genes that are activated in response to a variety of environmental stimuli. Some of these plants could be used in agriculture, to warn of the presence of insect pests, diseases, and so on. Others could be designed to detect chemical warfare agents or anthrax or even land mines—given that chemicals from land mines leak out of the soil. The researchers have received a grant of $3.5 million from the Defense Advanced Research Projects Agency to pursue this "sentinel garden."

Tremendous Strides in Food Safety

The food chain . . . has benefited from a new tracking method called the Pulse Outbreak system, which is coordinated by the Centers for Disease Control in Altlanta, Ga. "We have made tremendous strides in identifying food borne outbreaks using this system. We can now identify outbreaks that might have been isolated and far-flung. It has also helped us identify novel sources of outbreaks—like cantaloupe and tomatoes. We never thought of fresh fruit as being carriers of pathogens, but now, for example, we have put in HACCP [Hazard Analysis and Critical Control Points] programs for juices," notes [food safety program director Jenny Scott].

Another potential bright spot in food safety . . . comes shining through from the University of Florida, in Gainesville, and Douglas L. Archer, a professor in the food science and human nutrition department. He suggests that the freezing process itself seems to be a positive factor that can kill or weaken many micro-organisms, and he urges that more research be done to determine what combination of freezing temperatures and thawing are most lethal to the most deadly pathogens.

Michael Hartnett, *Frozen Food Age*, July 2003.

In Albany, California, scientists at the ARS Produce Safety and Microbiology Research Unit of the Western Regional Research Center are similarly using jellyfish genes as "bioreporters" to study the attachment of food-poisoning bacteria to animal surfaces (such as poultry skin) and crops (including leaves and roots). In one area of study, microbiologists Robert Mandrell, William Miller, and their colleagues have chosen to work with *Campylobacter*, which is a group of bacterial species that can infect humans and animals. According to the CDC, these bacteria are a common cause of diarrhea and affect two million people per year in the United States.

The ARS researchers have inserted fluorescence-imparting jellyfish genes into the DNA of *Campylobacter* cells, with each gene controlled by a promoter. In some experiments, the genes were continually activated so that the bacteria produced a steady fluorescent glow under UV illumination. The researchers were able to color code various strains of *Campylobacter* to emit yellow, green, or blue-green light. By this approach, they found that multiple strains of *Campylobacter* can coexist as aggregates on chicken skin.

In further investigations, the researchers have been linking the jellyfish genes to a variety of other promoters in *Campylobacter* DNA. In these cases, the genes are activated only in response to certain signals from the microbial cells, generated when the bacteria stick to poultry skin or grow within the chicken. By this approach, the scientists should be able to identify the particular promoters that are turned on and then to infer how various bacterial genes may be involved in an infection of the chicken. After that, they will look for ways to block the attachment or growth of the bacterial cells.

Biochip Sensors

Microbiologist Arun Bhunia, an associate professor of food science at Purdue University, has spent the past 12 years studying one of the deadliest of foodborne pathogens, a bacterial species named *Listeria monocytogenes*. Although only certain strains of the bacteria are pathogenic and cause only about 2,500 cases of food poisoning in the United States each year, the fatality rate is as high as 20 percent, according to the CDC. The main victims are people with an undeveloped or weak immune system, such as infants, the elderly, and HIV-infected individuals.

If a person eats food contaminated with a pathogenic strain of *Listeria*, the bacteria attach to the intestinal cells and penetrate the cell membrane. If the person's immune system cannot stop them, they may move to another organ, such as the liver, damaging it. Some potent strains can penetrate the blood-brain barrier, causing encephalitis and death.

Bhunia's aim is to build highly sensitive devices to detect the bacteria and to find ways to prevent the microbes from causing illness. For this purpose, he has been collaborating with other researchers in the Departments of Food Science, Agricultural and Biological Engineering, and Electrical and Computer Engineering at Purdue. Together they are developing a biochip sensor that can rapidly detect small numbers of the bacteria.

The scientists have succeeded in attaching lab-grown mouse antibodies on a tiny silicon chip, smaller than a postage stamp. A sample of food being tested is then placed on the chip. If pathogenic *Listeria* cells are present in the food sample, they bind to the antibodies on the chip and give a signal alerting the user that the food is contaminated.

"It takes just 100–1000 *Listeria* organisms to make a person sick," says Bhunia. "Our device is 100 percent accurate in detecting just 50 organisms." He believes that the biochip could ultimately be part of an inexpensive, handheld device that could be used on a farm, at a food-processing plant, or in a grocery store. He and his colleagues hope to develop similar sensors to identify other food contaminants as well. In recognition of the significance of his contribution, Bhunia was honored with an award from Purdue University [in 2003].

Irradiation Is a Hot Topic

[In] May [2003] the First World Congress on Food Irradiation was held in Chicago, Illinois. Addressing the congress, Elsa Murano, undersecretary for food safety at the U.S. Department of Agriculture (USDA), said that food irradiation is "the single most effective tool in killing foodborne pathogens." Another speaker, Gerald Moy, a scientist with the World Health Organization's Programme of Food Safety, called food irradiation "one of the most significant contributions to public health" since the introduction of pasteurization of milk.

Food irradiation is a technology by which food is briefly treated with ionizing radiation—such as X rays, gamma rays, or electron beams—as a means to eliminate or reduce the numbers of bacteria, parasites, molds, and insects associated with the food. The radiant energy breaks up molecular bonds in the DNA of these organisms, causing them to die or making them unable to reproduce. The radiation dosage varies with different types of food.

Some groups have raised a number of concerns regarding irradiated food. Does the food become radioactive? Is it safe to eat? Does it lose nutritional value? In response, several government agencies—particularly the FDA, USDA, and CDC—have reassured consumers that, based on extensive experimentation and testing, irradiated food is safe for human consumption and does not become radioactive or lose nutritional value. It is acknowledged that irradiation may lead to some changes in the food, similar to alterations caused by cooking, but to a lesser extent.

Both the FDA and USDA have approved a variety of foods (including meats and produce) for treatment by radiation. At the same time, they have cautioned that the principles of hygiene and safe-handling techniques must be applied to irradiated as well as un-irradiated foods, to prevent subsequent contamination. Many grocery stores and restaurants in this country are providing irradiated meats, fruits, and vegetables. Consumer acceptance, however, is still slow in coming.

In the meantime, at the University of Wisconsin-Madison, Ferencz Denes is applying his expertise in the new field of plasma-aided manufacturing to the area of food safety. He has shown that if food and food-processing equipment are treated with plasma, which is a stream of electrically charged particles, their surface properties are altered and they become resistant to bacteria.

"You could sterilize milk, water, seeds, fruits, vegetables, and even hard-to-clean conveyor belts by this method," says Michael Pariza, director of the Food Research Institute and chairman of the Department of Food Microbiology and Toxicology at the University of Wisconsin-Madison. This method would reduce the need for pesticides, which have troublesome side effects on humans and wildlife. Prototypes of the devices needed for this technique are now being made and several processes to be used in the devices have already been patented, notes Pariza. . . .

The Challenges

For all these methods, one challenge is to find the proper agents and conditions that will do the job without significantly changing the appearance, texture, taste, and nutritional value of the food. A second challenge is to find techniques that combine speed with efficacy, while keeping costs down. Yet, in light of the power of newly designed diagnostic equipment and novel approaches to eliminate harmful microbes and chemicals, scientists are providing us with valuable ways to enhance the safety of our world's food supplies.

"We need a holistic review of the current food production system, not an unwavering faith in the technological god."

New Technologies Do Not Prevent Food-Borne Illness

Monique Mikhail

New technologies are not the answer to the problem of food safety, argues Monique Mikhail in the following viewpoint. For example, corporate factory farms, which focus on high-volume production and profit, create sick animals and filthy meat, pollute the surrounding environment, and threaten rural economies and human health. Then, Mikhail reports, instead of addressing these root causes of food-borne illness, many companies use irradiation to sterilize their dirty meat—a process which in itself produces toxins that are not safe for consumption. Rather than rely on technology, consumers must educate themselves and demand that their government establish a healthy food production system, she concludes. Mikhail is an organizer in the Stop Food Irradiation Program.

As you read, consider the following questions:

1. According to Mikhail, why are the animals in factory farms fed antibiotics?
2. What are cyclobutanones, according to the author?
3. In Mikhail's opinion, what are some positive alternatives to the industrial food production system?

Monique Mikhail, "Is Your Food at Risk?" *Left Turn*, August/September 2003, pp. 58–60. Copyright © 2003 by *Left Turn*. Reproduced by permission.

How many times in the last year have you heard about E.Coli, Salmonella, or Listeria? Media hype would have you believe that people are dropping like flies just from eating dinner. But, rarely are the true sources of food-borne illness revealed. As meat recalls increasingly flood the news, people's fear of bacteria escalates and companies clamor, "We can solve our food safety problems with more, better, MY technology!" But in the whirl of hype, deceptive labeling and impenetrable Food and Drug Administration (FDA) regulations, the consumer is left confused. The wrong questions are being asked.

Why is our food not safe to begin with? And, if technology brought us to a system that produces unsafe food, why is more technology the answer? We need a holistic review of the current food production system, not an unwavering faith in the technological god.

Factory Farms

Within the last 20 years, the industrialization of the US meat industry has created "factory farms" the size of small cities. These "factory farms," also called Confined Animal Feeding Operations (CAFOs), emphasize high volume production and profit with little regard for humane animal treatment, human health, safe food, the environment, or the neighboring rural economy. Thousands of animals are packed into these facilities with little or no access to sunlight, fresh air, or room for natural movement, often wallowing in their own excrement. Because these unsanitary and confined living conditions make the animals sick, they are fed antibiotics (an estimated 70% of all antibiotics in the US) to promote growth and keep them "healthy."

Factory farms also have adverse effects on surrounding areas. The concentrated putrid waste from these factory farms fouls neighboring rivers, streams and wells. The stench travels for miles and lowers property values. Family farms are being forced out of business in droves, devastating rural economies, because they cannot compete with giant agribusiness companies. For example, 98% of all poultry is now produced by corporations.

These animals, covered in filth, are then processed in plants with ever-increasing line speeds that slaughter up to 140 chickens per minute and 400 cows per hour. Maintaining humane practices and clean meat is virtually impossible. And yet, due to industry-influenced legislation, the US Dept. of Agriculture's ability to effectively regulate and inspect has been restricted to the point of paralysis.

Industry's Solution

Instead of reassessing the causes of food-borne illness, meat companies are searching for a tool to reduce their liability without reducing profits or restructuring. Because food irradiation kills the bacteria that is harbored in the feces, urine, pus and other contaminants on meat, it enables companies to mask dirty meat while providing an additional processing step in which another industry can squeeze dollars from consumers. Under the auspices of being a "safe" choice, consumers can purchase meat containing "sterilized" feces for 20–30 cents more per pound.

But what does irradiation really do? Irradiation exposes food to a dose of energy equivalent to millions of chest X-rays. The process can be accomplished by one of three technologies: gamma rays (nuclear material), X-rays, and electron beam or "e-beam" (electrons moving close to the speed of light). Regardless of whether ionizing radiation comes from radioactive materials or "e-beams," its effect on food is the same; the only difference is how the radiation is produced.

Irradiation disrupts everything in its path, depleting nutrients and causing the creation of new chemicals—some of which do not naturally occur in food (called unique radiolytic products) and never studied by the FDA for safety. Research dating to the 1950s has revealed a wide range of problems in laboratory animals that ate irradiated foods, including premature death, cancer, stillbirths, genetic damage, organ malfunctions, stunted growth and vitamin deficiencies. Recent studies by the Federal Research Center in Germany found that one of these by-products, called cyclobutanones, promotes the cancer-development process in rats, and cause genetic and cellular damage in human and rat cells.

Irradiation proponents claim that the nutritional changes in food caused by irradiation are minimal, but the facts prove otherwise. Research has found that irradiation destroys up to 95 percent of the vitamin content in food. A 2002 study also showed that irradiated ground beef contains higher levels of *trans* fatty acids, which have been linked to higher levels of LDL ("bad") cholesterol and increased incidence of coronary heart disease.

Irradiation and Globalization

Because irradiation advances the consolidation and industrialization of our food supply, it is a technology that cannot coexist with local small-scale sustainable agriculture. Irradiation increases the shelf-life of food, thereby allowing further distance shipping and encouraging the globalization of our food. When production is shifted overseas where labor is cheaper and environmental protections are often more lax, companies increase profits while American farmers suffer.

Potential Dangers of Irradiated Food

[There] is the potential for chromosome damage in people who consume irradiated foods. Many in vitro and experimental studies have been performed, but there are only 2 relevant human studies, one carried out in India and one in China. In the Indian study, which was conducted in the mid-1970s, malnourished children were fed traditionally processed wheat or fresh or stored irradiated wheat; after a relatively short period of time, those fed fresh irradiated wheat showed chromosome breaks that were not found in children who were fed wheat that had not been irradiated or irradiated wheat that had been stored.

This study has been harshly criticized because of the small number of children it included and the methods that were used in conducting the study. These criticisms are valid, but the study still raises disturbing questions about possible genetic damage.

Donald B. Louria, *Clinical Infectious Diseases*, August 1, 2001.

Farmers of the global south also suffer. In the spring of 2002, the US Department of Agriculture legalized irradiation for imported fruit and vegetables. Multinational corporations are using their influence in global trade negotiations to push irradiation as a solution to the invasion of non-native fruit flies and other insects, which are considered "barriers to trade" under the WTO [World Trade Organization]. Wide-scale use of irradiation will therefore only intensify the current trend of converting farming communities in developing nations into monoculture cash croplands.

Why would government agencies approve this questionable technology? Unfortunately, research shows major flaws in the approval process. In the history of researching irradiation, much of it conducted by the government, raw data indicating that irradiated food may not be safe for consumption has been downplayed, ignored, and misrepresented. For example, in legalizing food irradiation, the US Food and Drug Administration (FDA) neglected to determine a level of radiation to which food can be exposed and still be safe for human consumption, which federal law requires, and relied on only seven of over 400 studies for approval. Furthermore, the FDA and USDA have never publicly addressed the new toxicity information found in European research about a class of chemicals formed during irradiation called cyclobutanones.

Labeling

Due to poor sales, the food irradiation industry has attempted for the past five years to force the FDA to change the labeling regulations for irradiated foods. Foods that are irradiated and sold in stores in the United States are required to display the radura, the international symbol for irradiation, and carry the phrase "treated with radiation" or "treated by irradiation." But there are major loopholes. Processed foods containing irradiated non-meat ingredients are exempt, as are irradiated foods served in restaurants, schools, hospitals, and nursing homes.

Due to a provision in the 2002 Farm Bill that the food irradiation industry lobbied for, the USDA has chosen to purchase irradiated food for the National School Lunch Program beginning in January 2004. Nowhere in the world has there been a mass feeding of irradiated food to children over a prolonged period of time. In the history of irradiation research, there has only been one study of the effects of irradiated food consumption on human children.

A chromosome abnormality called polyploidy—which has

been associated with leukemia and direct exposure to radiation—was detected in malnourished children who ate recently irradiated wheat. This is significant, considering that the schoolchildren most likely to consume a high percentage of their daily food intake from the school meal programs are already undernourished. Children are also more susceptible to toxic substances in their environment because they eat, drink and breathe three times as much as adults, pound for pound.

Irradiated food is also making its way to college dining halls. College campuses are major sources of income for large foodservice corporations, like SYSCO and Alliant, who have already begun incorporating irradiated food into their supplies. Irradiated food does not have to be labeled when served in cafeterias at educational institutions!

Fortunately, consumers are becoming more aware of the problems with our industrial food system. We are beginning to ask the right questions and re-examine our agriculture system to envision positive alternatives. For example, sales of organic food are increasing over 25% annually, and programs like Community Supported Agriculture (CSA)—where consumers can buy a "share" of a farmer's crop at the beginning of the summer and then have fresh local produce delivered to them weekly throughout the growing season—are expanding.

Farmers Markets and Buy Local campaigns are also rising in popularity. Programs such as Farm to School—developing programs with schools and colleges to contract with local growers instead of contracting out to massive foodservice companies—and school gardens help teach children to have a connection with their food as they learn where it comes from and how to support their local farm economies. Communal gardens in cities contribute to community development, education, and environmental awareness.

Every bite you take is a political act. Corporations have derailed both consumers and family farmers and accelerated our world down the path of excessive processing. Americans have ceded control of the very substances that sustain our lives. It is time to get back on track. We must ask critical questions, hold our government accountable to the citizens it purportedly represents, and work together toward a safe, healthy, and sustainable food system.

Periodical Bibliography

The following articles have been selected to supplement the diverse views presented in this chapter.

John Collinge	"Mad Cow Disease: The British Lesson," *World Press Review*, March 2004.
Holly Dressel	"A Better Life for Hogs," *Yes! A Journal of Positive Futures*, Spring 2004.
Susan Friedberg	"Starved for Reform," *Washington Post National Weekly Edition*, January 19–25, 2004.
Jessica Hankinson	"Designing Foods to Prevent Diseases," *World & I*, May 2004.
Michael Hartnett	"Making Food Safer: New Initiatives, New Investments, and a Renewed Commitment to Food Safety by Companies Throughout the Food Chain Are Producing Positive Results," *Frozen Food Age*, July 2003.
Julie Light	"Working to Keep Antibiotics Working: Can the Superbugs Be Stopped?" *Multinational Monitor*, January/February 2004.
Donald B. Louria	"Food Irradiation: Unresolved Issues," *Clinical Infectious Diseases*, August 1, 2001.
Steven Milloy	"Don't Have a Cow," *Los Angeles Times*, January 2, 2004.
Ralph Nader	"In the Public Interest: Regulating Meat Products," *Liberal Opinion Week*, January 5, 2004.
John E. Peck	"The Mad Cows Finally Come Home," *Z Magazine*, March 2004.
Abigail Trafford	"Cow Madness Is Overblown," *Washington Post*, February 13, 2001.
University of California, Berkeley, Wellness Letter	"Update on Irradiation," December 2003.

For Further Discussion

Chapter 1

1. Jennifer Brower and Peter Chalk argue that the overuse and misuse of antibiotics is increasing the risk of the spread of dangerous diseases. David Baltimore contends that extensive media reports often cause public overreaction to news about emerging diseases. After reading these two viewpoints, which do you believe poses the greater threat to the public: the misuse of antibiotics or the potential for media-driven panic over diseases? Defend your answer with citations from the chapter.

2. In their respective viewpoints, Richard Danzig and the editors of *Hospital Infection Control* each cite the mailed anthrax attacks of 2001 as an example to back up their arguments. In your opinion, which of these authors uses the anthrax example to better effect? Why?

3. What arguments, examples, and statistics does Rian Malan use to support his contention that the extent of AIDS in Africa has been greatly exaggerated? Which do you find most convincing? Which do you find least convincing? Do you agree with his conclusion that the international "AIDS establishment" has intentionally overstated the threat of AIDS to win more funding for its organizations? Why or why not?

Chapter 2

1. George W. Bush contends that emergency funding from the United States will help to curtail the AIDS crisis in several African and Caribbean nations. What serious flaw does Greg Behrman see in the plan proposed by Bush? After reading the viewpoints in this chapter, what do you believe would be the best approach to combating the global AIDS epidemic?

2. The editors of *Christianity Today* maintain that encouraging abstinence and marital faithfulness is the most effective way to reduce the spread of AIDS in Africa. Why does Ndivhuwo Masindi take issue with this strategy? How effective do you think her proposals would be in curtailing the spread of AIDS in Africa?

3. Both Rod Dreher and Terence P. Jeffrey argue that fighting AIDS requires the condemnation of people who engage in high-risk behavior, while Peter Aggleton, Arleen Leibowitz, Stephanie Taylor, and Jonathan Fielding contend that improved education and access to testing are more effective approaches. Do these authors harbor irreconcilable philosophical differences, or might

there be a way that their suggestions could be combined into one public health policy? Explain your answer.

Chapter 3

1. Barbara Loe Fisher maintains that parents should be allowed to excuse their children from mandated immunization programs. What does Arthur Allen find disturbing about the growing number of families who avoid vaccinations? Whose viewpoint do you most agree with, and why?

2. Kelly Patricia O'Meara reports that vaccines containing the mercury-based preservative Thimerosal may be linked to the recent dramatic increase in autism. Marie C. McCormick, a spokesperson for the Institute of Medicine, announces that there is no connection between vaccines and autism. Does McCormick's argument effectively refute O'Meara's? Why or why not?

3. Ronald D. Harris is a colonel in the U.S. Air Force Reserve. John Richardson is a Gulf War veteran. How relevant do you think their backgrounds are to their arguments concerning the vaccination of military personnel? Does the fact that they may have a personal stake in the issue lend credence to their arguments or provide grounds for questioning their objectivity, in your view? Explain.

Chapter 4

1. Joel Bleifuss argues that U.S. government agencies have failed to acknowledge that eating the meat of cattle infected with mad cow disease could cause a fatal neurological disease in humans. Steven Milloy maintains that there has been no conclusive evidence linking mad cow–infected beef to human illness. Do you agree with Bleifuss that the U.S. government is protecting the beef industry at the cost of human health, or do you believe, as Milloy contends, that the mad cow scare is mostly media hype? Use evidence from the viewpoints to support your answer.

2. Which of the arguments for or against food irradiation made by B.G. Scott and Monique Mikhail do you find most convincing? Which do you find least convincing? After reading their arguments, would you be more or less likely to purchase food that has been irradiated? Explain.

Organizations to Contact

The editors have compiled the following list of organizations concerned with the issues debated in this book. The descriptions are derived from materials provided by the organizations. All have publications or information available for interested readers. The list was compiled on the date of publication of the present volume; the information provided here may change. Be aware that many organizations take several weeks or longer to respond to inquiries, so allow as much time as possible.

American Council on Science and Health (ACSH)
1995 Broadway, Second Floor, New York, NY 10023-5860
(212) 362-7704 • fax: (212) 362-4919
e-mail: acsh@acsh.org • Web site: www.acsh.org

ACSH is a consumer education consortium concerned with, among other topics, issues related to health and disease. ACSH publishes the periodical *ACSH News* and other informational pamphlets and articles such as "Vaccinations: What Parents Need to Know," and "Stamping Out Polio." The ACSH Web site includes links to recent articles, editorials, and speeches on diseases, food safety, and terrorism.

American Foundation for AIDS Research (AmFAR)
120 Wall St., Thirteenth Floor, New York, NY 10005-3908
(212) 806-1600 • fax: (212) 806-1601
Web site: www.amfar.org

The American Foundation for AIDS Research is a nonprofit organization dedicated to the support of HIV/AIDS research, AIDS prevention, treatment, education, and the advocacy of sound AIDS-related public policy. AmFAR's mission is to prevent the disease and death associated with HIV infection and to protect the human rights of those threatened by the epidemic of HIV/AIDS. The Web site includes links to recent news articles and information on global initiatives and antiretroviral therapies.

Biohazard News (BHN)
925 Lakeville St., PO Box 251, Petaluma, CA 94952
e-mail: info@biohazardnews.net
Web site: www.biohazardnews.net

BHN is a volunteer-run organization dedicated to providing the public with timely information about the threat of biological terrorism, which it believes to be one of the most serious threats to America's national security. It publishes a free newsletter and maintains a Web site that includes interviews and information on biological weapons and terrorist groups.

Centers for Disease Control and Prevention (CDC)
1600 Clifton Rd., Atlanta, GA 30333
(404) 639-3311
Web site: www.cdc.gov

The CDC is the government agency charged with protecting the public health of the nation by preventing and controlling diseases and by responding to public health emergencies. Programs of the CDC include the National Center for Infectious Diseases, which publishes *Addressing Emerging Infectious Disease Threats: A Prevention Strategy for the United States* and the journal *Emerging Infectious Diseases*. The CDC Web site includes an index of links to fact sheets, frequently asked questions, press releases, and articles on diseases, prevention efforts, and immunization.

Family Research Council
801 G St. NW, Washington, DC 20001
(202) 393-2100 • fax: (202) 393-2134
Web site: www.frc.org

The Family Research Council promotes the traditional family unit and the Judeo-Christian value system. The council opposes the public education system's tolerance of homosexuality and condom distribution programs, which its members believe encourage sexual promiscuity and lead to the spread of AIDS. It publishes numerous reports from a conservative perspective, including the monthly newsletter *Washington Watch* and the bimonthly journal *Family Policy*.

Federation of American Scientists (FAS)
1717 K St. NW, Suite 209, Washington, DC 20036
(202) 546-3300 • fax: (202) 675-1010
e-mail: fas@fas.org • Web site: www.fas.org

The Federation of American Scientists is a privately funded, nonprofit organization engaged in analysis and advocacy on science, technology, and public policy for global security. Its Chemical and Biological Arms Control Program works to prevent the development and use of biological weapons. FAS publishes the quarterly journal *Public Interest Report*. The federation requests that students and other researchers first investigate the resources available on its Web site, such as the paper *Biological Weapons and "Bioterrorism" in the First Years of the 21st* Century, before requesting further information.

Focus on the Family
8605 Explorer Dr., Colorado Springs, CO 80920
(719) 531-3400 • (800) 232-6459
Web site: www.family.org
Focus on the Family promotes traditional Christian values and strong family ties. It publishes the monthly magazine *Focus on the Family* for parents, educators, and children. The organization has also produced *Sex, Lies, and . . . the Truth*, a video that encourages abstinence and criticizes safe-sex messages, which its members believe increase the spread of AIDS. Publications are available from its Web site.

Food and Drug Administration (FDA)
5600 Fishers Ln., Rockville, MD 20857-0001
(888) 463-6332
Web site: www.fda.gov
Part of the U.S. Department of Health and Human Services, the FDA's mission is to promote and protect the public health by helping safe and effective foods, drugs, and medicines reach the market in a timely manner, and to monitor such products for continued safety after they are in use. The administration's work is a blending of law and science aimed at protecting consumers. The FDA publishes the magazine *FDA Consumer* as well as various government documents, reports, fact sheets, and press announcements.

Food Safety Consortium (FSC)
110 Agriculture Building
University of Arkansas, Fayetteville, AR 72701
(501) 575-5647 • fax: (501) 575-7531
e-mail: fsc@cavern.uark.edu • Web site: www.uark.edu/depts/fsc
Congress established the Food Safety Consortium, consisting of researchers from the University of Arkansas, Iowa State University, and Kansas State University, in 1988 through a special Cooperative State Research Service Grant. It conducts extensive investigation into all areas of poultry, beef, and pork meat production. The consortium publishes the quarterly *FSC Newsletter.*

Global Vaccine Awareness League (GVAL)
25422 Trabuco Rd., Suite 105-230, Lake Forest, CA 92630-2797
e-mail: Michelle@gval.com • Web site: www.gval.com
The league is a nonprofit organization committed to educating parents and concerned citizens about the potential risks and serious side effects of vaccines. It publishes a newsletter, fact sheets about vaccines, books, videotapes, and pamphlets such as *Exemp-*

tion Information for U.S. States and *Disease—The Power That Heals the Body.*

International Vegetarian Union (IVU)
PO Box 9710, Washington, DC 20016
(202) 362-8349
e-mail: vuna@ivu.org • Web site: www.ivu.org
The International Vegetarian Union is a nonprofit organization, which advocates animal welfare and humanitarian and health objectives. It publishes the annual *IVU News* and makes available on its Web site articles concerning food safety issues from affiliate vegetarian organizations.

Johns Hopkins Center for Civilian Biodefense Strategies
111 Market Place, Suite 830, Baltimore, MD 21202
(410) 223-1667 • fax: (410) 223-1665
Web site: www.hopkins-biodefense.org
The center is an independent, nonprofit organization of the Johns Hopkins Bloomberg School of Public Health and the School of Medicine. It works to prevent the development and use of biological weapons and to advocate medical and public health policies that would minimize the damage of biological warfare. It produces the journals *Biodefense Quarterly* and *Biosecurity and Bioterrorism.* Articles, reports, and other resources are available on its Web site.

National Association of People with AIDS (NAPWA)
1413 K St. NW, Washington, DC 20005
(202) 898-0414 • fax: (202) 898-0435
e-mail: info@napwa.org • Web site: www.napwa.org
NAPWA is an organization that represents people with AIDS and HIV. It sponsors programs that develop positive leadership in people living with HIV and AIDS, advocates for the needs of those living with HIV or at risk of becoming infected, and works with the growing movement of people with AIDS throughout the developing world. The organization publishes informational material, including the periodic e-mail based newsletter *Positive Voice Update.*

National Cattlemen's Beef Association (NCBA)
5420 S. Quebec St., Greenwood Village, CO 80111-1905
(303) 694-0305 • fax: (303) 694-2851
e-mail: cattle@beef.org • Web site: www.beef.org
National Cattlemen's Beef Association is the marketing organization and trade association for America's one million cattle farmers and ranchers. Its Food Safety library publishes the quarterly *Food*

and Nutrition newsletter, the fact sheet "Progress in Food Safety: Toward a Safer Beef Supply," and the booklet *Playing It Safe.*

National Coalition for Adult Immunization (NCAI)
4733 Bethesda Ave., Suite 750, Bethesda, MD 20814-5278
(301) 656-0003 • fax: (301) 907-0878
e-mail: ncai@nfid.org • Web site: www.nfid.org/ncai

The NCAI is a nonprofit organization composed of more than ninety-five professional medical and health care associations, advocacy groups, voluntary organizations, vaccine manufacturers, and government health agencies. The common goal of all members is to improve the immunization status of adults and adolescents to levels specified by the U.S. Public Health Service. Annually, the NCAI publishes the *Resource Guide for Adult and Adolescent Immunization* and spearheads the National Adult Immunization Awareness Week campaign in October. The organization also publishes a newsletter and papers such as *A Call to Action: Improving Influenza and Pneumococcal Immunization Rates Among High-Risk Adults* and *Standards for Adult Immunization Practice.*

National Foundation for Infectious Diseases (NFID)
4733 Bethesda Ave., Suite 750, Bethesda, MD 20814
(301) 656-0003 • fax: (301) 907-0878
e-mail: info@nfid.org • Web site: www.nfid.org

The foundation is a nonprofit philanthropic organization that supports disease research through grants and fellowships and educates the public about research, treatment, and prevention of infectious diseases. It publishes a newsletter, *Double Helix*, and its Web site contains a "Virtual Library of Diseases."

National Institute of Allergy and Infectious Diseases (NIAID)
Vaccine Research Center, Building 40, Room 4502
31 Center Dr., MSC 2520, Bethesda, MD 20892-5717
(301) 496-1852 • fax: (301) 496-5717
e-mail: gnable@nih.gov • Web site: www.niaid.nih.gov

The institute, one of the programs of the National Institutes of Health, supports scientists conducting research on infectious, immunologic, and allergic diseases that afflict people worldwide. Vaccines and emerging diseases constitute two of the NIAID's main areas of research, and many materials are available from the NIAID on these topics, including *Understanding Vaccines* and *Emerging Infectious Diseases Research: Meeting the Challenge*. The Web site includes a searchable database with links to articles on diseases, vaccine research, and bioterrorism.

National Vaccine Information Center (NVIC)
421-E Church St., Vienna, VA 22180
(800) 909-7468 • (703) 938-0342 • fax: (703) 938-5768
Web site: www.909shot.com
Founded in 1982, the NVIC is the oldest and largest parent-led organization dedicated to the prevention of vaccine injuries and deaths through public education. The center provides assistance to parents whose children have suffered vaccine reactions and promotes research to evaluate vaccine safety and effectiveness as well as to identify factors which place individuals at high risk for suffering vaccine reactions. The NVIC supports the right of citizens to exercise informed consent and make educated, independent vaccination decisions for themselves and their children. The center distributes information on vaccine safety and on reporting adverse effects after vaccination, and it publishes the book *The Consumer's Guide to Childhood Vaccines*.

Safe Tables Our Priority (STOP)
PO Box 4352, Burlington, VT 05406
(802) 863-0555 • fax: (802) 863-3733
e-mail: mail@safetables.org • Web site: www.stop-usa.org
Safe Tables Our Priority is a nonprofit organization devoted to victim assistance, public education, and policy advocacy for safe food and public health. STOP's mission is to prevent unnecessary illness and loss of life from pathogenic food-borne illness. STOP's publications include newsletters, policy statements, testimonies, and press releases. The organization also offers several pamphlets including "What Is Foodborne Disease?" and "The Problem Is Unsafe Food," as well as a report, *Why Are People Still Dying from Contaminated Food?*

Sexuality Information and Education Council of the United States (SIECUS)
130 W. Forty-second St., Suite 350, New York, NY 10036-7802
(212) 819-9770 • fax: (212) 819-9776
e-mail: siecus@siecus.org • Web site: www.siecus.org
SIECUS is an organization of educators, physicians, social workers, and others who support the individual's right to acquire knowledge of sexuality and who encourage responsible sexual behavior. The council promotes comprehensive sex education for all children that includes AIDS education, teaching about homosexuality, and instruction about sexually transmitted diseases. It publications include fact sheets, the bimonthly *SIECUS Report*, and the books *Winning the Battle: Developing Support for Sexuality and HIV/AIDS Education* and *How to Talk to Our Children About AIDS*.

Bibliography of Books

Karen M. Booth   *Local Women, Global Science: Fighting AIDS in Kenya.* Bloomington: Indiana University Press, 2004.

Chris Bull, ed.   *While the World Sleeps: Writing from the First Twenty Years of the Global AIDS Plague.* New York: Thunder's Mouth Press, 2003.

Lincoln Chen, Jennifer Leaning, and Vasant Narasimhan, eds.   *Global Health Challenges for Human Security.* Cambridge, MA: Harvard University Press, 2003.

Michelle Cochrane   *When AIDS Began: San Francisco and the Making of an Epidemic.* New York: Routledge, 2004.

Rob DeSalle, ed.   *Epidemic! The World of Infectious Diseases.* New York: New Press, 1999.

Hung Fan, Ross F. Coner, and Luis P. Villarreal   *AIDS: Science and Society.* Boston: Jones and Bartlett, 2004.

Robert H. Gates   *Infectious Disease Secrets.* Philadelphia: Elsevier, 2003.

Victor Gentle and Janet Perry   *Plagues.* Milwaukee, WI: Gareth Stevens, 2001.

Larry O. Gostin   *The AIDS Pandemic: Complacency, Injustice, and Unfulfilled Expectations.* Chapel Hill: University of North Carolina Press, 2004.

Rebecca Hohlstein   *Food Fight: The Battle to Protect Our Food and Water Against Terrorism.* Madison, WI: Goblin Fern Press, 2003.

George C. Kohn   *Encyclopedia of Plague and Pestilence: From Ancient Times to the Present.* Rev. ed. New York: Facts On File, 2002.

Felissa R. Lashley and Jerry D. Durham, eds.   *Emerging Infectious Diseases: Trends and Issues.* New York: Springer, 2002.

Warren Leon   *Is Our Food Safe?* New York: Crown/Three Rivers Press, 2002.

Howard Markel   *When Germs Travel: Six Major Epidemics That Have Invaded America Since 1900 and the Fears They Have Unleashed.* New York: Pantheon Books, 2004.

Gary Null and James Feast   *Germs, Biological Warfare, Vaccinations: What You Need to Know.* New York: Seven Stories Press, 2002.

Michael T. Osterholm and John Schwartz	*Living Terrors: What America Needs to Know to Survive the Coming Bioterrorist Catastrophe.* New York: Dell, 2001.
Andrew T. Price-Smith	*The Health of Nations: Infectious Disease, Environmental Change, and Their Effects on National Security and Development.* Cambridge, MA: MIT Press, 2002.
Andrew T. Price-Smith, ed.	*Plagues and Politics: Infectious Disease and International Policy.* New York: Palgrave, 2001.
Nicholas Regush	*The Virus Within: A Coming Epidemic.* New York: Plume, 2001.
Aviva Jill Romm	*Vaccinations: A Thoughtful Parent's Guide—How to Make Safe, Sensible Decisions About the Risks, Benefits, and Alternatives.* Rochester, VT: Healing Arts Press, 2001.
Diane Rozario	*The Immunization Resource Guide: Where to Find Answers to All Your Questions About Childhood Vaccinations.* Burlington, IA: Patter Publications, 2001.
Maxine Schwartz	*How the Cows Turned Mad.* Berkeley: University of California Press, 2003.
Susan Scott	*Biology of Plagues: Evidence from Historical Populations.* New York: Cambridge University Press, 2001.
Arvind Singhai and W. Stephen Howard	*The Children of Africa Confront AIDS: From Vulnerablity to Possibility.* Athens: Ohio University Press, 2003.
Mary Ellen Snodgrass	*World Epidemics: A Cultural Chronology of Disease from Prehistory to the Era of SARS.* Jefferson, NC: McFarland, 2003.
Charlotte A. Spencer	*Mad Cows and Cannibals: A Guide to the Transmissible Spongiform Encephalopathies.* Upper Saddle River, NJ: Prentice-Hall, 2003.
John Stauber	*Mad Cow USA.* Monroe, ME: Common Courage Press, 2003.
Ronald O. Valdiserri, ed.	*Dawning Answers: How the HIV/AIDS Epidemic Has Helped to Strengthen Public Health.* New York: Oxford University Press, 2003.
Mark Jerome Walters	*Six Modern Plagues and How We Are Causing Them.* Washington, DC: Island Press/Shearwater Books, 2003.
Sarah B. Watstein and Stephen E. Stratton	*The Encyclopedia of HIV and AIDS.* New York: Facts On File, 2003.

Index

would curtail AIDS epidemic, 93–98
genetically engineered (GE) foods,
  165–66
Gerberding, Julie, 44–45
Global AIDS Fund, 81
Global Eradication Program (World
  Health Organization), 156
globalization
  food irradiation and, 190–91
  has facilitated spread of infectious
    disease, 17–19
global warming, as factor in disease
  spread, 16
Gottlieb, Jim, 138
Graham, Franklin, 90
Green, Edward C., 90
Greenfield, William, 155
Groopman, Jerome, 12
Gupta, Geeta Rao, 117
Guyana, HIV/AIDS in, 61

Hammer, Scott, 62
Harris, Ronald D., 152
Hartman, Todd, 170, 171
Hartnett, Michael, 182
Health for All 2000 accord, 19–20
herd immunity, 123
Heymann, David, 45
Ho, Mae-Wan, 165
Hodge, James G., 12
homosexuals, promiscuity among,
  108–109
  social condemnation as answer to,
    111–12
Hospital Infection Control (journal), 37
human immunodeficiency virus. *See*
  AIDS/HIV

immunization. *See* vaccination
India, HIV/AIDS in, 25, 59
infectious disease(s)
  emerging amd reemerging, 17
  factors in spread of, 17
    globalization, 17–19
    global warming, 23–24
    medical practices, 19–21
    social/behavioral patterns, 24–26
    urbanization, 21–23
  media exaggerates threat of, 27–31
    con, 16–26
informed consent, mandating
  vaccination is violation of, 131–32
Institute of Medicine (IOM), report on
  anthrax vaccine, 157
Intergovernmental Panel on Climate
  Change, 23
irradiation of food, 184–85
  dangers of, 189–90, 191–92

Islam, A.Q.M. Serajul, 59–60

Jaffe, Harold, 63
Jefferson, Thomas, 155
Jeffrey, Terence P., 103
Jenner, Edward, 155
*Journal of American Physicians and
  Surgeons,* 141
Judd, Ali, 62

Kaiser Family Foundation, 104
Keating, Susan Katz, 35
Keenlyside, Richard, 60
Keffeler, Kathy, 138
Kennedy, Ted, 35
Koppel, Ted, 31

Lacy, Rachel, 159, 160
land use changes, 26
Latin America
  cholera epidemic in, 23
  HIV/AIDS in, 60–61
Leahy, Patrick, 34
Lederberg, Joshua, 23
Legionnaires' disease, 11, 17, 19, 26
Leibowitz, Arleen, 99
Lim Hng Kiang, 48
Linden, Frank, 22–23
Listeria monocytogenes, 183–84
listeriosis, 176
Louria, Donald B., 190
Lumpkin, Murray, 51
Lyme disease, 11, 26

mad cow disease (bovine spongiform
  encephalitis, BSE)
  cause of, 168
  is not a serious public threat, 174–77
    con, 167–73
  U.S. cases of, 169–70
Mad Cow U.S.A. (Stauber), 172
Madonna, 67–68
Malan, Rian, 65
malaria
  antibiotic-resistant, 38
  global warming and, 24
Mandrell, Robert, 182
Marlink, Richard, 81
Marsh, Richard, 169, 170
Martin, Ray, 91
Masindi, Ndivhuwo, 93
Matambanadzo, Bella, 96
May, Thomas, 161
McCarrick, Theodore, 90
McCormick, Marie C., 147
McCullagh, Declan, 47
measles, cases before/after vaccine
  approval, 136